THE POWER OF EXHIBIT MARKETING

THE POWER OF EXHIBIT MARKETING

Barry Siskind

Self-Counsel Press
(a division of)
International Self-Counsel Press Ltd.
U.S.A. Canada

Printed in Canada

First edition: September 1990; Reprinted: April 1991
Second edition: January 1993; Reprinted: August 1994
Third edition: January 1996
Fourth edition: September 1997

Canadian Cataloguing in Publication Data

Siskind, Barry, 1946-
   The power of exhibit marketing

   (Self-Counsel business series)
   Previous eds. have title: The successful exhibitor's
handbook.
   ISBN 1-55180-121-3

   1. Exhibitions. 2. Selling. I. Title. II. Title:
The successful exhibitor's handbook. III.Series.
T396.S572 1997   659.1'52   C97-910706-7

Research material published by the Center for Exhibition
Industry Research (CEIR) is reproduced with permission.
Copies of the full report are available for sale from CEIR —
call (301) 907-7626.

Self-Counsel Press
(a division of)
International Self-Counsel Press Ltd.

1704 N. State Street   1481 Charlotte Road
Bellingham, WA 98225   North Vancouver, BC V7J 1H1
U.S.A.   Canada

CONTENTS

WORKSHEETS

SAMPLES

FIGURES

ACKNOWLEDGMENTS

No book becomes reality without the help and encouragement of lots of people. I look at the list of names of people who have offered their assistance and I am overwhelmed. Without them this book and my career would not be what they are today.

My first debt is the thousands of workshop participants who have offered suggestions, personal stories, advice, and encouragement for me to keep doing what I do. To all of you — thank you.

To the people in the industry who have taken time from their busy schedules to offer advice, complete questionnaires, or share their war stories: Ray Argyle, Harley Austin, Diane Blair, Enzo Calisi, David Carter, Gerald Chopik, Jim Creighton, Jon Denman, Deborah Dugan, Ann Dutchburn, Sheila Edmonson, Michael Fenton, Peter Giffin, Ronald Gooch, Robert Grainger, Gary Hanna, Hank Hartloper, David Hiu, Maureen Hizaka, Carol Hopper, John Houghton, Peter Jaroslawski, Geoffrey Jones, Pamela Kanter, Donna Leigh, Paul Lorimer, Patricia Marshall, Warren Maybee, Blair Melton, Blake Mintz, Sandra Morrow, Don Obert, Kathy O'Hara, Megan Parry, Peter Phillips, Charles Pollacco, Dawn Raider-Kapansky, Lorraine Reardon, Derek Retter, Michel Samson, Liliana Sarda, Anita Schachter, Helmuth Schroeter, Jennifer Sickinger, Steven Sind, Dana Walker, Glenn Waterman, Janice Waugh, Gregory Weeden, Ray Weind, Fred West, and Gordon Wheeler.

To Cliff Hand for his help with the first edition of this book. Much of the work we did "back then" still inspires me.

To the folks at Self-Counsel who have worked with me during the past few years. Particular thanks to Ruth Wilson, Lori Ledingham and Roberta Barens.

My special thanks is to Barbara Siskind, my partner in business and in life. I dedicate this book to her for all the usual reasons plus one more.

Barry Siskind

PREFACE

Welcome to the exciting world of trade and consumer shows.

Selling effectively in international and domestic markets, through the medium of trade and consumer shows, requires the use of skills and techniques that have been developed and improved over many centuries. In fact, many of the basic selling skills used in the colorful eastern markets of antiquity are still widely used today.

Successful selling is an exercise in effective communications between two or more human beings. While the product or service being sold is important, the first priority in any sales effort is to establish a communications link between the buyer and seller. Whether it is the ancient trader in the marketplace calling, "Have I got a deal for you!" or the sophisticated sales representative of today questioning a new prospect on his or her immediate needs, the purpose of the verbal exchange is to establish communication — to create a desire for more information that will eventually lead to a sale.

The Power of Exhibit Marketing (formerly *The Successful Exhibitor's Handbook*) has been written and designed as a reference book for managers and staff who participate in trade and consumer shows, both at home and abroad.

According to *Trade Show Weekly,* there are more than 10,000 annual shows in North America. Over 1,000,000 companies participate in these shows and spend in excess of $20 billion exhibiting their wares.

This is indeed big business, yet many companies take a seat-of-the-pants approach to their show participation, especially where support staff is concerned. The principles outlined in this book apply to every staff member who participates in a show. Each must understand the importance of his or her individual contribution.

The contents of this book should be required reading for every person in your company who has any part in your show activities.

To help both neophyte and experienced show participant get the most out of this book, it has been organized into three sections:

PART I — BEFORE THE SHOW: An essential ingredient of a successful show is careful planning and preparation well before show deadlines.

PART II — AT THE SHOW: The all-important skills of selling and working the booth must be properly understood.

PART III — AFTER THE SHOW: All of the time and money spent on the show is wasted if you don't have a properly planned and executed follow-up procedure and an in-depth analysis of the show results.

Use the forms illustrated in the book as part of your own planning and execution procedures. Following the step-by-step guides should result in more profitable and enjoyable shows for all involved. Even though you may not shout the same slogans as the eastern trader did, you will be able to give a professional equivalent of the old "come-on," with high expectations and a smile!

PART I
BEFORE THE SHOW

1
WHY EXHIBIT?

a. *EXHIBITING IN THE MARKETING MIX*

When it comes to marketing your products or services, you have a plethora of tools. Marketing can be achieved through TV, radio and print advertising, special events, collateral material, telemarketing, the Internet, field sales, or trade and consumer shows. An impressive list to choose from, but which is the most effective method to work with? Do all the tools yield a similar outcome? What part do trade and consumer shows play in the equation?

The challenge of choosing the right balance is what marketing is all about. While this book will not deal with the challenges and benefits of all forms of marketing, we will examine, in detail, the exhibit function and its place in the overall marketing mix.

Exhibits began thousands of years ago, in ancient times when they were called bazaars — forerunners to the modern general merchandise show. Here, merchants and farmers met to sell their wares. Since these humble beginnings, exhibitions have matured. During the last half of this century we have seen a proliferation of highly specialized shows. Some focus on the needs of re-sellers and some on the end users. As we approach the next millennium the lines that differentiate these two types of shows are fading. Some trade shows that profess to cater to re-sellers, agents, and distributors also encourage public attendance, while other shows are created primarily for the end user.

Trade shows have been around for ages, so why all the hype now? The answer is simple. Before the dawn of TV, trade shows were the marketing method of choice. During the past 50 years we switched allegiance, and radio, TV, and newspapers became the more accepted marketing tools. Exhibiting took a back seat.

Exhibiting became a victim of familiarity. Apathy slowly crept in. The new media was glitzy, glamorous, and caught our corporate imagination. Trade shows were old, boring, and lacked pizzazz. All that has changed. Trade shows around the globe have become sophisticated, high-impact marketing tools. The glitz and glamour have returned but to a more serious audience. Trade shows are no longer a place for amateurs; they are a forum for sophisticated exhibitors who understand the real power of exhibiting.

In The Power of Exhibitions I, a survey conducted by Simmons Market Research, the results are conclusive (see Table #1). From the point of view of the shows' visitors, exhibitions are the number one source of information with which to make purchasing decisions.

There is a myth that people attend shows because they have nothing better to do, they want to take a day off work, or they just want to collect show freebies. However, the numbers don't back up this myth. The numbers clearly indicate that shows attract visitors who are well targeted and serious. Visitors attend shows to conduct business. If marketers choose the right show (see chapter 2) — the show that attracts their target

Table #1
Purchasing information:
how useful is your marketing method?

Trade shows	91%
Articles in trade publications	86%
Friends/business associates	83%
Directories and catalogues	72%
Manufacturers' representatives	69%
Ads in trade publications	66%
On-site visits	64%
Conferences and seminars	59%
User groups	41%
In-house purchasing departments	40%
Outside consultants	39%
Retail/sales staff	23%
Newspapers	22%
Other	2%

Source: CEIR, Power of Exhibitions I,
conducted by Simmons Market Research Bureau, 1993

audience — you would think exhibitors would be breaking the doors down to participate. But it is not as simple as that.

While marketing executives authorize significant expenditures, they are plagued with questions:

- What is our return?

- What do we really get from our exhibit program?

- Why should we continue to participate?

- What can we do to be successful or even more successful?

- How does our exhibit program fit into our overall scheme of things?

- Are our exhibits fully integrated into our sales and marketing program?

According to Stephen Sind, president of the Centre for Exhibition Industry Research (CEIR), the reason most marketers have difficulty answering these questions is that they "put the cart before the horse." Marketers get caught up in the razzle-dazzle of shows and the pizzazz of their physical exhibits. It is not uncommon to see an exhibitor purchase a new booth and then ask the question, "What am I going to do with it?"

As a consultant, I have faced this dilemma many times. There have been many clients who had embarked on an extensive exhibit program and ignored some of the basic questions. This book will be your journey through the maze of questions and decisions you will need to face. Before we begin the journey, let's see if there is a place for exhibiting in your marketing mix.

CEIR regularly conducts research initiatives for the exhibition industry. A recent major study was its Power of Exhibitions. In this two-part study, the centre was able to draw four major conclusions:

— Exhibitors who set measurable and quantifiable goals are more successful than those who do not.

— Marketers allocate more dollars to shows than to other marketing tools, except for direct sales.

— Exhibitions make "cents."

— Exhibitors with an integrated plan are more successful.

1. Exhibitors who set measurable and quantifiable goals are more successful than those who do not

An obvious statement? It seems natural to set an objective before any business activity. However, there is an overwhelming number of exhibitors who do not take the time to identify a clear, measurable, and realistic objective for their exhibiting. Setting clear objectives for an event is the foundation of exhibiting success for several reasons.

(a) If you don't know where you are going, your chances of getting there are pretty slim.

(b) Knowing what you are trying to achieve allows you to focus your resources, time, and message for maximum results.

(c) Knowing what you want to achieve allows you to gauge your results.

Later in this chapter, you will learn how to set good objectives for your next exhibit.

It is evident by statistics shown in Table #2 that exhibitions have been proven a more successful method of reaching objectives than other marketing tools.

The results shown in Table #2 do not mean you shouldn't allocate resources to other marketing methods. However, exhibitions are part of the marketing mix

Table #2
Effectiveness of marketing methods in reaching objectives

	Exhibitions	Advertising	Direct Mail	Public Relations
Generate sales leads	39%	27%	20%	13%
Taking orders	12%	5%	8%	8%
Introduce new products/services	42%	24%	28%	14%
Promote brand image	42%	43%	19%	19%
Promote company awareness	33%	32%	22%	24%
Enter new markets	28%	25%	24%	15%

Source: CEIR, Power of Exhibitions II,
Deloitte & Touche Consulting Group, 1996

and should be given their rightful place. By understanding how an exhibit can move you forward, you will also understand the importance an exhibit holds in your overall marketing efforts.

2. Marketers allocate more dollars to shows than to other marketing tools, except for direct sales

The Power of Exhibitions II, a second survey conducted by CEIR, found that sales and marketing executives placed exhibitions second in their allocation of marketing dollars: exhibitions were allocated 14% of total budget (see Table #3).

An interesting observation is that while the direct sales force is deemed indispensable, it is more costly to

Table #3
Budget allocation for marketing methods

Exhibitions	14%
Direct sales	47%
Advertising	11.5%
Direct mail	9%
Public Relations	6.5%
Telemarketing	5%

Source: CEIR, The Power of Exhibitions II, 1956,
Deloitte & Touche Consulting Group

maintain. A CEIR research report (report SM17) indicates that the cost to make contact with a prospect in the field is $277, versus $162 for the same quality contact made at an exhibition. The report continues with the estimated cost of $977 to close a field lead versus $550 to close a show lead. Does all this mean we should eliminate our direct sales force and concentrate primarily on exhibitions? That would be a tough sell in any business. However, these numbers justify putting exhibitions in second place when allocating marketing resources.

The beauty of exhibiting is that it gives your customers something other marketing methods lack — an experience. Visitors have an opportunity to experience your products, services, programs, and personnel first hand. Visitors want to touch, see, hear, taste, and smell, and at a show, they have an opportunity to explore more of these senses than they do with any other form of marketing. Marketers who understand this will develop their booths to give visitors a maximum experience. These findings are consistent when the statistics for the high-tech, food and beverage, manufacturing, and health care sectors are examined (see Table #4).

3. Exhibiting makes "cents"

If there were no payoff, marketers would not be taking exhibiting seriously. The real payoff of a show is found in the actions taken by visitors (see Table #5).

For visitors, a show is a one-stop shopping experience. All the solutions and information they need are found under one roof, and they can see it all in a concentrated period. The show provides an opportunity for visitors to experience the products and services

Table #4
Allocation of marketing budget by sector

	High-tech	Food/Beverage	Machine tool manufacturing	Health care
Direct sales	41%	42%	47%	41%
Exhibitions	18%	17%	19%	21%
Advertising	14%	16%	14%	12%
Direct mail	11%	6%	7%	9%
Public relations	4%	7%	8%	8%
Telemarketing	6%	4%	4%	5%

Table #5
Actions taken by visitors

Signed a purchase order	26%
Found at least one new supplier	77%
Asked for a price quote	76%
Requested a sales rep visit	51%
Conducted comparative shopping	94%

*Source: CEIR, Power of Exhibitions I,
Simmons Market Research Bureau*

they have not been exposed to previously. According to a 1994 survey by Exhibit Surveys for the CEIR, nine out of ten visitors had not received a personal sales call from the exhibitor.

For the visitors, then, shows are a valuable opportunity for many reasons. As seen in Table #6, decision makers use shows as a forum for finding new products and services, as well as for keeping up with the latest trends and directions.

Another CEIR report (report AC/RR 1150) found that 51% of show visitors attend only one show. This

Table #6
Decision makers' perception of trade shows

	% "generally agreeing" with statement
Saves my company time and money	85%
Brings me up-to-date	83%
Allows me to be productive	82%
Provides an invaluable opportunity	80%
Helps me decide	79%
Relied on by my company to keep up with current trends	70%

Source: CEIR, The Power of Trade Shows I, report PT2, prepared by Simmons Market Research Bureau

figure points to one thing — shows attract serious visitors, which translates to serious opportunities for the savvy exhibitor.

Visitors are clear about what they want. Table #7 highlights the three most important benefits for a visitor at a show.

And finally, exhibitions really do make "cents" and rank a close second to direct/field sales in importance in the selling process (see Table #8).

4. Exhibitors with an integrated plan are more successful

Exhibitors who integrate other marketing components into their exhibition program increase visitor attraction. Renting booth space and erecting a great-looking display is not enough. Successful exhibitors use a number of integrated marketing tools to reach their potential customers (see Tables #9 and #10).

An integrated blend of direct sales, advertising, direct mail, public relations, telemarketing, and exhibiting will produce the best overall results.

Marketers should think of their exhibitions as one further opportunity to reinforce corporate messages and their overall marketing plan. Various elements can be used in the exhibiting effort. These elements form part of the pre-show, at-the-show, and post-show follow-up.

It is important that your staff understands how your exhibition plans fit into the overall marketing mix and that they have the necessary skills to execute a successful

Table #7
Information most important to decision makers

In-depth product information	67%
Information to help evaluate products and services	62%
Comparison information on competitive products	59%

*Source: CEIR, Power of Exhibitions I,
Simmons Market Research*

Table #8
Marketing methods used in the selling process

Direct/field sales	85%
Exhibitions	81%
Advertising	66%
Direct mail	62%
Public relations	58%
Telemarketing	38%

*Source: CEIR, Power of Exhibitions II, 1996,
Deloitte & Touche Consulting Group*

Table #9
Integrating components increases attraction
of your target audience

Advertising	+46%
Sponsorships	+104%
Press conferences	+77%
Hospitality functions	+86%

*Source: CEIR, Power of Exhibitions II, 1996,
Deloitte & Touche Consulting Group*

Table #10
Converting target audience to qualified leads
increases when integrating components

Pre-show promotion	+50%
At-show promotion	+62%
Staff training	+68%

*Source: CEIR, Power of Exhibitions II, 1996,
Deloitte & Touche Consulting Group*

show. Without well-trained staff, all the marketing in the world goes out the window.

Exhibitions are an important part of the marketing mix. Visitors come to buy, and exhibitions provide a useful source of purchasing information. To maximize the benefit, both visitors and exhibitors need to have a clear understanding of the importance of shows. Experience shows that those marketers who understand this information, obtain commitment from all levels of their corporation, and have a good focused objective, stand out as the winners.

Trade and consumer shows have regained their past power. They have become a place for serious decision making. Shows are no longer a place for amateurs; rather, they are a place for sophisticated exhibitors. Read on and travel through the maze of decisions you will be faced with and learn how you can become a truly successful exhibitor.

b. BEING FOCUSED IS THE KEY TO EXHIBITING SUCCESS

Visitors come to trade shows with anticipation. They look for new products and services, attend the workshops, and network with colleagues, but above all, they try to find vendors who understand their needs.

Sounds like a reasonable expectation. However, finding exhibitors who really understand the benefits of exhibiting and have mastered the skills of turning those benefits into realities can be rare.

A successful show, like any well-executed marketing exercise, starts with a carefully thought-out plan of action. Such a plan gives direction to the whole effort, sets goals, and creates a yardstick to measure results.

A natural beginning is to ask the question, "Why should I exhibit? What is in it for me, my company, and those salespeople I am going to take off the road for several days?"

These are questions that you should answer before spending time planning to participate in a show. The answer to these questions helps you decide whether to participate.

It all starts with a clear understanding of the benefits. Exhibitors invest in shows as an opportunity to do everything from selling products and services to recruiting dealers and distributors. In fact, on a closer look, there are one hundred reasons to participate in a show.

Generally objectives can be found in two broad categories: sales and communication. Sales objectives are clearly those that lead to selling your products and services. Communication objectives are those that help express ideas, concepts, programs, or marketing messages to the show attendee. We could argue that all objectives are sales since that is the essence for all activities — to sell or persuade a visitor to adopt our product, idea, service, technology, or to use the information you are passing along to them to change a lifestyle. However, the shrewd exhibitor understands that to make the correct exhibiting decisions, the lines between sales and communication must be clearly drawn.

Coming to grips with all these reasons can be an onerous task. On further examination, the one hundred objectives can be subdivided into six helpful categories: introduction, enhancement, education, networking, supporting, and finding. Understanding the area of interest will help you focus your show activities and will help make the differentiation between sales and communication clearer. In fact, having a specific objective is the guideline for every show decision, as well as being a tool that helps booth staff concentrate on those things that are most important.

Investing in a show without a specific objective is like flying a plane without a flight plan. You might as well not exhibit at all. A brief look at the six categories is the beginning point.

The first category gives the exhibitor the opportunity to **introduce**. Introducing a new product or service, new personnel, or a new company to a market are objectives that fit well with visitors' expectations. Studies have shown that 51% of show visitors identify finding new products and services as their primary reason for attending a show.

For many exhibitors, letting your market know who you are and what you are all about is the primary objective. Objectives that **enhance** your image in a market fall into the second category. An image is crucial to everyone, but many exhibitors ignore the impact their visual image will have on their potential market.

The next category includes objectives that **educate**. Often a face-to-face explanation will help your customer understand new applications or increased efficiencies that using your products and services may achieve. A show is a perfect place to educate customers.

Much of your business will be found away from the booth. Understanding how to uncover hidden opportunities is found in the category of **networking**. Shows are the granddaddy of networking events and the well-prepared exhibitor will plan time to participate in as many show activities as possible.

Supports for a sales territory, industry, or personnel are found in the next category. A strong commitment will help convince prospects that you are serious about doing business. The rewards in this category are long term, but just as important as some shorter term objectives.

Finally, there are those objectives that help exhibitors **find** things. Shows are a cornucopia of opportunity. The aware exhibitor has a chance to find new business opportunities, personnel, products, and markets. As an exhibitor, if you have a business opportunity, proper signage in your booth will let the world — including other exhibitors — know.

Each of these 100 objectives may fall into one of more of these six categories, depending on how you as the exhibitor interpret this information.

Understanding the importance of setting show objectives and focusing on the category that makes most business sense to your business is the key to exhibiting success. Try to get too much from your booth and your chances of failure are enormous. Focus on one category that will help you advance your business and your chance of success grows. Trade shows do work. Start with an understanding of what you want and then focus your energies on everything that will ensure you get it.

The list of 100 objectives follows. Each has been identified as either sales (s), communication (c), or both. Read through the list and identify those objectives that are valid for your next show.

1. Sell products and services on the show floor (s)

2. Gather qualified leads for post-show company follow-up (s)

3. Introduce new products or services to a market (s)

4. Demonstrate new products or services (s)

5. Demonstrate new uses of existing products or services (c)

6. Give your audience an opportunity to meet the experts (c)

7. Give your CEO an opportunity to meet your customers (c)

8. Meet your buyers face to face (c)

9. Open new markets (s)

10. See buyers not usually accessible to sales personnel (s)

11. Find the decision makers (s)

12. Understand your prospects' decision making process (s)

13. Support the decision influencers (s)

14. Be compared to the competition (s)

15. Learn about your competition (c)

16. Solve customers' problems (s)

17. Obtain feedback on new products (c)

18. Obtain feedback on existing products (c)

19. Conduct market research (c)

20. Find dealers, reps, and agents (s)

21. Educate dealers, reps, and agents (c)

22. Find personnel (c)

23. Educate personnel (c)

24. Develop leads for dealers, reps, and agents to follow up (s)

25. Reinforce company image to a market (c)

26. Establish a new company image with a market (c)

27. Create customer lists (s)

28. Support your industry (c)

29. Reach your customers at a low cost per call (s)

30. Highlight new products and services to the media (c)

31. Highlight new company initiatives to the media (c)

32. Distribute product samples to your market (s)

33. Diffuse customer complaints (c)

34. Reinforce your marketing plans (s)

35. Distribute product or service information (s)

36. Conduct a sales meeting (c)

37. Support corporate theme programs (c)

38. Introduce a new promotional program (c)

39. Introduce a new service (s)

40. Educate your customers (c)

41. Introduce new techniques (c)

42. Re-position your company in a market (c)

43. Change the perception of your company in a market (c)

44. Expose new employees to an industry (c)

45. Learn new industry trends (c)

46. Network with colleagues (c)

47. Network with industry professionals (c)

48. Showcase new products and services (s)

49. Establish business relationships with international buyers (s)

50. Introduce new products and services (s)

51. Support dealers, reps, and agents (s)

52. Demonstrate your commitment to a market (c)

53. Gather competitive intelligence (c)

54. Attend the show's functions (c)

55. Influence customer attitudes (s)

56. Create high rate-of-investment opportunities (s)

57. Develop strategic relationships (c)

58. Find new business opportunities (c)

59. Uncover joint venture opportunities (c)

60. Unveil licensing opportunities (c)

61. Find new business location possibilities (s)

62. Determine the effectiveness of marketing and promotion campaigns (c)

63. Host special industry hospitality events (s)

64. Have company experts showcased at seminars and workshops (c)

65. Market research for future product developments (s)

66. Introduce new production methods (s)

67. Directly influence decision makers (s)

68. Reduce sales costs (s)

69. Entertain special customers (s)

70. Distribute promotional tools (s)

71. Influence industry trends (c)

72. Have a portable showroom (s)

73. Introduce product uses through audio or video programs (s)

74. Interact with a highly targeted audience (s)

75. Build sales force morale (c)

76. Give prospects opportunities to experience your product/service (s)

77. Open doors for future sales calls (s)

78. Understand/uncover your customer attitudes (c)

79. Present live product demonstrations (s)

80. Introduce support services (s)

81. Give the behind-the-scenes personnel a chance to meet the customer (c)

82. Create a three-dimensional sales presentation (s)

83. Introduce community awareness initiatives (c)

84. Open foreign markets quickly (s)

85. Find other exhibiting opportunities (s), (c)

86. Find ways of reducing exhibiting costs (c)

87. Develop new marketing techniques (c)

88. Create an image for your company (c)

89. Demonstrate non-portable equipment (s)

90. Overcome unfavorable publicity (s), (c)

91. Publicize company associations (c)

92. Explain the effects of corporate changes (c)

93. Bring your senior management closer to your customer (c)

94. Shorten the buying cycle (s)

95. Relate to the competition (s)

96. Generate excitement for new products/ services (s)

97. Increase corporate profitability (c)

98. Enhance word-of-mouth market (s)

99. Explain new programs (c)

100. Round out corporate marketing mix (c)

c. PLAN YOUR SHOW GOALS

Use Worksheet #1 to set your goals and rank them in order of importance.

Now, take another look at your list of goals. As you scan them, pick out one or two that are crucial for you to attain. These goals should be your main reasons for your doing the show in the first place. Once you have identified these crucial goals, place an asterisk beside them. They are now your primary goals for the show and all of your planning should be oriented toward achieving them.

If you try to achieve everything at a show, your chances of success are greatly reduced. The "shotgun" approach dilutes your efforts and leaves insufficient time to concentrate on the goals that really matter.

To achieve maximum success, all your efforts should be focused on your primary reasons for doing the show — this includes your booth, promotion, budget, and people. If, at the show, you can attain some of your other goals, consider that icing on the cake.

The secret to successful exhibiting is to remain focused.

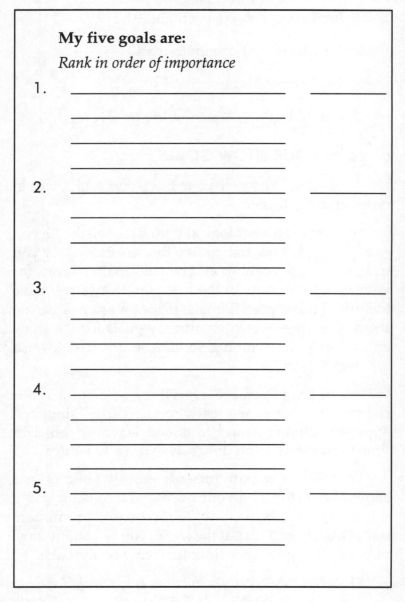

My five goals are:

Rank in order of importance

1. _____ _____

    _____

    _____

    _____

2. _____ _____

    _____

    _____

    _____

3. _____ _____

    _____

    _____

    _____

4. _____ _____

    _____

    _____

    _____

5. _____ _____

    _____

    _____

d. MEASURING YOUR GOALS

You now have a good idea of what your goals should be, but how specific can you be at this time? Can you measure them? Are they realistic?

Goals that cannot be measured are not really goals at all, they are vague hopes. Goals that cannot be realized only lead to frustrated staff and lost opportunities. The selection of realistic and measurable goals calls for thorough research and unbiased analysis of your market and the demographics of the shows you plan to participate in.

The reason for measuring goals is to provide a guide for your future show activities. For this reason, your goals should be short term even if your product has a long-term sales cycle.

For example, a heavy equipment manufacturer may have an 18-month sales cycle but can't wait $1\frac{1}{2}$ years to decide whether the show was worthwhile. In this case, the goal might be measured by the number of qualified leads received at the show.

When you are introducing a new product or demonstrating a specialized product, your immediate goal may not be sales. In this case, your goal could be the number of demonstrations given, or acceptance by a major purchaser or government laboratory for testing.

If you are exhibiting for the first time, your primary goals may be one of the following:

(a) To create awareness of your products and your company

(b) To get a feel for the local market

(c) To find a reliable local agent or distributor

Goals should be quantifiable to be of value. If your goal is sales, measuring is easy — you count the number of orders or sales leads. In other cases, measuring goals can seem very difficult. For example, a participant in one of my trade show seminars sold his products through a network of dealers. His goal was to create an image for his company. When asked how he would know when an image had been created, he replied, "When people see my product and understand how it can help them."

"So, if you can show your product to people who have never seen it before, and they understand how it can help them, will you have satisfied your image need?" I asked.

"Sure," he replied, "I want as many people as possible to know about my product."

"How many?"

"All 12,000," he replied.

When developing a measurement for your goals, ask yourself this question: "How will I know when I have it?"

The obvious answer is, "When I get sales."

Every goal is eventually measured in terms of sales — after all, sales are the purpose for your business activities. If you have created a positive image in your industry, people will be more inclined to do business with you. However, the timing can be a problem. Many exhibitors do not realize sales from a particular show immediately: they may not come until 12, 18, or 24 months after the event. Such long delays in realizing sales can put the exhibitor at a disadvantage. Long before all results from one show are realized, you will be faced with a decision — should you do the show again?

You should never do a show out of habit; you should do it for profit. Profit from a show is more than long-term sales. Think of profits in the short-term: gathering a number of qualified leads to work on, acquiring or maintaining a certain image in your industry, gathering market intelligence, or finding good representatives for your products.

Sales results give an absolute measurement, but you'll often have to focus on short-term results for your immediate, post-show profit calculations. That is, if your next show gets you 50 qualified leads based on your history, how many of them will result in business? What is the amount of your average opening order? Now you can equate a short-term goal to money.

So, back to the question: "How will I know when I have got it?" The answer lies in asking people. Conduct on-site or post-show surveys asking people if you have met your objective. In the example above, it would mean asking 12,000 people if they now understood how the product would help them. If you were able to ask them all, and if all said yes — you have succeeded.

More than 12,000 people is a measurable goal, but far from realistic for several reasons, which are discussed in the following section.

e. SETTING REALISTIC GOALS

Setting realistic goals is just as important to your success as selecting the right goals. If your targets are too low or too easy to attain, you won't feel challenged to perform and you'll probably miss a number of opportunities. On the other hand, if your targets are too high or too demanding, you'll have a disgruntled sales force and a bad feeling about the show.

How do you set realistic goals?

Let's continue the story of our manufacturer, who was trying to create an image for his company.

Reference to the demographics for the show, provided by the show manager, showed that approximately 12,000 visitors attended the show last year. Of these, about 8% were plant engineers — the industry group the manufacturer wished to reach. A discussion with the show manager and several exhibitors led to the conclusion that this manufacturer could expect 30% to 35% of the visiting plant engineers to pass through his booth — approximately 300 leads. After further discussion, he decided that perhaps half of those would be unfamiliar with his product line.

So now, our manufacturer has his goal: to demonstrate his product to 150 new qualified prospects. By setting this goal, he has taken a giant step toward having a very successful trade show.

Even though the manufacturer is happy with these figures, there's still one very important question that hasn't been asked: Is the booth staff capable of handling 150 demonstrations during show hours?

Assuming that each salesperson is able to make two presentations during each hour of duty, a 25-hour show would require three salespeople on duty at all times to meet the goal.

Whether your target is the number of sales leads, visitors contacted, or sales volume generated, the figures that you come up with should be carefully researched. They should relate directly to the number of visitors that you can realistically expect to stop at your booth, and the booth should be staffed properly to meet your goal.

If you don't have previous experience with a particular show to enable you to come up with reliable estimates, then talk to show management, other exhibitors, competitors, suppliers, and customers.

f. RANKING YOUR GOALS

By now, you probably have between five and ten items on your list of goals. One or two should stand out as being the prime reasons for exhibiting. For example, if your purpose for exhibiting is to attract representation, then you must ask whether the show will help you find a good agent. Most of your efforts should go toward reaching this goal. If, for any reason, a show does not offer the chance to achieve your primary goals, you should not use that particular show.

The balance of your list of goals should be ranked in order of importance. This calls for impartial judgment and an honest appraisal of the significance of each goal. Some you may have to be prepared to sacrifice in favor of those higher up on your list.

g. INDIVIDUAL GOALS

Once you have a clear set of goals that meet the criteria of measurability and realism, the next step is to translate them into personal goals for each member of your show staff. While your corporate goals give overall direction to your show efforts, personal goals act as motivators for each member of the show team.

The advantages of setting these individual show goals are:

(a) they serve as milestones for measuring individual progress,

(b) collectively, they serve as milestones for evaluating overall show performance,

(c) they can be tied into a reward system, and

(d) when monitored on a continual basis throughout the show, they give the exhibitor an opportunity to re-evaluate booth objectives at any time.

1. Milestones for individual progress

It's important for everyone in your booth to have a clear idea of what is expected of them. Too often, booth people do not know why they are there. Knowing their goals helps motivate them through the long show hours, helps keep them focused, and reduces the amount of wasted time.

2. Milestones for evaluating overall performance

In order to evaluate your show you need a measurable objective. Chapter 16 discusses show evaluation in more detail, but for now, keep in mind that the more effort you put into creating measurable goals, the easier it will be for you later when evaluating your results.

3. Reward systems

Exhibitors often set up systems that reward their staff for doing their job well. Bonuses, trips, dinners, entertainment tickets, and prizes can be tied easily to a measurable show objective.

4. Continual monitoring

Continual monitoring lets you take advantage of every show situation. Let's say that you have decided on a daily goal of 25 qualified leads but on the first day, you only get 10 leads. Does this mean it is a bad show? Maybe yes; maybe no. How can you tell?

If you set up milestones beforehand against which to check progress, you can easily monitor the efforts of your booth staff to make sure things are going as planned. On close examination you may find that you have a display problem, or your promotional material is not targeted properly, or perhaps your goal was wrong in the first place. If it is a booth, people, or promotional problem, you have until the show opens on the second day to fix it. If your goals are wrong, you may be able to change them or focus on your secondary goals. When you can't get what you originally wanted, look for alternatives, don't waste the rest of your show time complaining.

Personal goals can be broken down in several ways depending on the specific overall goal that you are trying to meet.

In the earlier example, the manufacturer's goal was to make 150 demonstrations during the 25 show hours. Individual goals could be set up as follows:

Each show day:

Number of demonstrations	50.0
Number of shifts	2.0
Demonstrations/shift	25.0
Number staff/shift	3.0
Demonstrations/person/shift	8.3

From this calculation we can assign an individual goal of 8.3 demonstrations per shift to each salesperson — a goal that is both measurable and realistic.

In the example, we have assumed equal traffic on each day of the show. In practice this may not be the case and staffing will have to be adjusted to take account of the historic traffic patterns of the particular show.

Once you have selected a show and have reliable demographic information, it is important that you get your staff involved as early as possible. Explain to them why you have chosen the particular show, what your corporate goals are, and how you plan to measure them.

h. CALCULATING REALIZABLE SHOW GOALS

Now it is time to consider the "how to" part of setting goals. There are two basic methods you can use: the short method and the long method. The short method is most useful when you are trying to evaluate the potential of several shows. It allows you to weed out shows that have little potential without wasting a lot of time on the exercise. Once you have shortlisted the shows that have potential, the long form should be used to make a more accurate assessment.

1. The short method

(a) Step 1

From information supplied by the show manager, extract the following:

(a) Total number of people expected to attend the show

(b) Total number who attended the last show

(c) Percentage of those attending that you estimate should be interested in your product (i.e., the people you want to meet)

(d) The total number of hours the show is open to visitors

(b) Step 2

From your own experience of past shows, estimate or calculate the following:

(a) Percentage of leads received that turn into firm orders

(b) The average size of the opening orders received

(c) Step 3

Using the figures obtained above, calculate the expected return on the show, as shown in Sample #1

2. The long method

The long method requires a careful analysis and a fair amount of research, but gives a more accurate estimate of the results to be expected from the show. The method is taken from Edward A. Ebb Jr.'s book, *Exhibit Marketing*, (McGraw Hill, 1987).

(a) Step 1

Obtain the figures for the total expected audience, as in the short method.

(b) Step 2

Determine how many visitors belong to groups that are not potential buyers. Subtract this number from the total attendance to get the number of potential buyers expected. The visitors' profile for previous shows should be available from the show manager or the audit agency if the show was audited. Figures from the agency should be more reliable, but you will have to use your own judgment in assessing the reliability of any figures you receive. If you have doubts, talk to other exhibitors — get their reactions.

You may also want to consider other attractions the show is offering. Some may attend just to hear a high-profile speaker or to see a specific demonstration.

Some of the groups you may identify as non-buyers and deduct from the total audience are spouses, students, press, guests, and others whose titles clearly eliminate them as potential buyers.

Sample #1
Using the short method to calculate show goals

Step 1:

Attendance	30,000
Interest level at 4% of 30,000	1,200
Total show hours	32

Step 2:

Percentage of leads converted	20%
Average opening order size	$500

Step 3:

Average number of leads per hour

$$1,200/32 = 37.5$$

(You must staff your booth to handle this level of activity)

$$20\% \text{ of } 1,200 \text{ leads} = 240$$

Expected return on the show = 240 x $500 or $120,000

(c) Step 3

Determine what percentage of the potential buyers will be interested in your products or services. In some cases it may be 100%, but in many others it will be considerably less. Not only must type of product or service be taken into account, so must other factors such as methods of marketing, product mix, size of company, etc. Each of these factors can limit the portion of the potential market that you can realistically expect to supply.

(d) Step 4

Assess the audience interest factor (A.I.F.) for your show. This is defined as the percentage of visitors who stop and obtain literature from at least 20% of exhibitors. Statistics from past shows give an A.I.F. of 57% for vertical or trade shows, and 48% for horizontal or consumer shows.

(e) Step 5

A percentage of those who stop by your booth will not be real buyers. This percentage is called the waste factor and includes those who are confused, lost, or only interested in gimmicks, premiums, and special demonstrations. This figure should be assessed with care as it can be as high as 25% or more of those that visit your booth.

(f) Step 6

Industry averages say that only 20% of contacts will result in sales. This is an average and may be different for your industry. Use your past experience to come up with a realistic figure for your industry.

Out of every ten contacts, the industry average breaks down as follows:

(a) Two contacts are not interested

(b) Four contacts are interested but not buyers

(c) Two contacts are buyers but leave no leads

(d) Two contacts are buyers and leave leads

(g) Step 7

The number of leads per hour as calculated in the short method is too simplified. As you are aware, there are periods when the show is very busy and the lead collection rate will be much higher. A more detailed explanation of the show patterns is examined in chapter 3 when we look at booth staffing. For now, use only the busy times of the show to calculate the number of opening hours. Ignore periods such as when a high profile speaker is scheduled.

(h) Step 8

Calculate the rate at which leads will be converted into sales. The Center for Exhibition Industry Research says that 40% of show leads buy within three months.

Sample #2 shows a calculation using the long method.

Sample #2
Using the long method to calculate show goals

Step 1: Total expected audience   30,000

Step 2: Past show analysis of non-buyers
Spouses	6,000
Exhibitors	1,000
Press, guests, students	<u>3,000</u>
Total non-specific	<u>10,000</u>
Total potential buyers	20,000

Step 3: Industry expectations
My products are used by 25% of the industry
25% of 20,000   5,000

Step 4: A.I.F. is 57% for vertical shows
57% of 5,000   2,850

Step 5: Waste factor is 25%
75% of 2,850   2,137

**Step 6: Leads per hour for an effective
total of 32 hours**
2,137 divided by 32   67

Step 7: 20% rule
20% of 2,137   427

Step 8: Calculate your quantifiable objective
If 40% buy within 3 months at an average
opening order of $3,000
427 x 40% x $3,000 = $512,400

2
PICKING THE RIGHT SHOW

Whether there is only one show, or several, that covers the market and audience you wish to reach, the procedures advocated in this chapter are equally applicable. After you have read this chapter, you should be able to make an informed decision about the potential value of any particular show that interests you.

During the last decade, the number of shows in North America has more than doubled. Today, there are over 10,000 shows of all kinds that you can visit each year, each with a character of its own.

Smaller, regional shows usually have promotion budgets that match their potential revenues. The big national and international shows require huge, up-front expenditures to promote them to their widely scattered audiences, as well as large staffs to run them.

In between these extremes are all kinds of shows, some well run, others not well run. Some have adequate budgets, others try to bootstrap themselves into a sound financial condition. Overseas shows have the added danger of unfamiliar territory.

How do you find the right show and check it out before investing your time and money in it? Preferably, you will follow the four stages discussed below:

(a) List and check suitable shows.

41

(b) Check demographics and facilities.

(c) Check the fit with your goals.

(d) Decide how much space to book.

Let's take a look at each of these stages in turn.

a. *LIST AND CHECK SUITABLE SHOWS*

The number of shows covered in your particular field will depend on the market you are trying to reach.

Several publishing companies issue annual directories that list trade and consumer shows. Some cover the domestic market only, others cover world markets. In these directories you'll find a lot of very useful information. Shows are usually listed by their industrial classification, location, number of exhibitors, type of show, number of visitors, total space available, and date. These directories should be your primary source of information. (See Appendix 1 for a list of directories.)

Secondary sources of information are your own trade magazines, trade associations (which often run their own trade shows), your customers, and local chambers of commerce.

Governments are also an important source of information. They maintain staff at home and abroad whose job it is to keep abreast of all commercial activities within their industrial or geographic sectors.

Once you have the list of available shows, you can quickly screen it for dates that conflict with other plans or are too close to allow adequate planning. For the remaining names on your list, a letter, facsimile, or phone call should quickly bring a brochure (and maybe a salesperson!) giving you full details of the show.

If the show has been established for a number of years and is growing, you can be sure the brochure will tell you so. It will also give you a list of exhibitors that have participated in previous shows. If you have any doubts, call up some of these exhibitors and ask for their opinions. You can learn a lot from a few simple inquiries that could save you thousands of dollars in wasted efforts.

If the show company is new or unknown to you, then a more thorough investigation is warranted. It is not unknown for shows to be canceled a few weeks before show time for lack of bookings or financial difficulties.

Do a credit check on the company. Ask the show manager for a list of exhibitors who have booked to date. If he or she balks, be suspicious. Phone some of the exhibitors on the show list — be sure their attendance is confirmed.

This may seem like a lot of work, but it is worth the effort when you consider the damage a canceled show might do to your marketing program. By then you could have wasted tens of thousands of dollars on preparation and promotion.

With your shortlist in hand and the show brochures set out around you, you can now proceed to the detail work of studying the demographics of each show.

b. CHECK DEMOGRAPHICS AND FACILITIES

There are two concerns here: first, the demographic profiles of both the visitors and the exhibitors, and, second, the type of show and facilities provided by show management. Both concerns are important. Here is a list of questions to which you should seek answers.

1. What type of show is it?

This may seem obvious, but there are some shows where the dividing line between a trade show and a consumer show gets blurred. If you are interested in selling only to the trade, then you may not want a show where the public is admitted at certain hours or on certain days. On the other hand, if you are exhibiting a consumer item at a trade show, you may welcome public attendance at certain times as a public relations gesture.

2. Is it regional, national, or international?

Regional shows cater to local markets and are promoted only to that market. National shows are promoted to draw attendance from across the nation. International shows are major events designed to attract a large contingent of foreign exhibitors and delegates. They are often coupled with high-profile workshops and seminars and are widely promoted and supported by the government or major industry associations of the host country.

3. What is the exhibitor profile?

An exhibitor profile is more than just a list of exhibitors — it is also a breakdown by industry segment (Standard Industrial Classification (SIC) codes, for example). Examine the list carefully. You want to know whether your competitors use this show to sell their wares or if they find some other show more effective. Are the major players represented?

4. What is the visitor profile?

Most show managers provide some form of visitor demographics — from raw numbers to detailed breakdowns by job function, job title, geographical location, and size of company. Your interest here is not only the total number of visitors to the show, but how many are potential buyers of your product, and, of that number, what percentage you can reasonably expect to pass through your booth.

5. How is the show being promoted?

Poor promotion usually results in poor turnout. Most show managers, if asked, will give you details of their promotion program. This should include direct mail, magazine and newspaper advertising, radio and TV spots, and trade association support. You may want to tie your own promotion into some of these programs, especially the pre-show issues that are often produced by related trade magazines.

6. What type of registration system is being used?

There are two aspects to registration systems. First, you want a system that gets visitors in with as little fuss as possible. Second, you need a system that records information for future use and incorporates some kind of retrieval system for use with sales leads. Many of the larger shows use embossed cards or imprinters to record sales leads. Others use codes on the visitor badges. If you expect a lot of leads at the show, then you should carefully consider the type of registration system in use.

7. Are there any other associated events?

Shows often have special events associated with them, such as receptions, awards banquets, high-profile keynote speakers, galas, media conferences, and seminar programs.

8. Is there a technical program?

In some industries, the technical program is a vital part of the show. In other cases, a show may be added on to a technical conference. In either case, the technical content is often the one reason that is given by visitors for attending. Departmental managers are often reluctant to let several of their staff take a day or afternoon off just to walk a trade show. On the other hand, permission to attend a seminar on a subject that is work-related is readily given.

9. What are the show amenities?

As an exhibitor, you may need special services such as compressed air. Is it readily available? What is the loading capacity of the floor? If you have a heavy exhibit, this could be important. What are your electrical power requirements?

How does the show facility cater to a large influx of visitors? Are the restaurant and washroom facilities adequate? Will visitors be encouraged to spend as long as possible at the show, or will they leave early in frustration or disgust?

10. What are the show regulations?

What are the regulations concerning the height and construction of exhibits? If you already have an existing booth, will it conform? Many regulations are dictated by local fire departments. Is your booth made of fire retardant materials? Other regulations cover the shape of your booth, the height of the sidewalls, blockage of the booths next to you, etc. It pays to read the show regulations very carefully, especially before you design a new booth or enter an unfamiliar show. Regulations are often very rigid and not always at the discretion of the show manager to change.

11. Are show layout and traffic patterns well designed?

The layout of the show can have a noticeable effect on the traffic patterns. As a newcomer to the show, you may not have much choice of booth location. Book early and state your preference as strongly as you can. If you don't want to be anywhere near your competition, let the show manager know.

Many shows try to group similar products together in well-marked locations. While this may put you near your competition, it does have the advantage of drawing all of the buyers of like products to the same area and increasing your exposure.

12. What shipping and receiving facilities are available?

You want your exhibit to arrive in good condition and in time to allow you to set it up properly. If you have a large piece of machinery, make sure that the loading dock and passageways can accommodate it. Beware the exhibition hall that has only one or two loading docks and gives priority to the official carrier! Be especially aware of facilities that are above the ground floor and require elevators. If the facility is a union shop, problems could arise through the use of non-union labor.

13. Is public transportation and/or parking available?

Nothing upsets visitors more than poor and expensive parking facilities. Easy, well-marked parking is a must. There should be good public transportation or a show shuttle bus to and from the exhibition hall.

Proximity to hotels and airports is also a consideration.

14. Are there prizes for best booth, etc.?

Many show managers organize prizes for best booth, best product, or best international exhibit. You should enter these if you can, for a win means extra publicity.

15. What media coverage will there be?

Check to see if the show manager plans to send out press releases to the local radio and TV stations and the daily papers. If you have an interesting product, you may be included in the show's promotion.

c. CHECK THE FIT WITH YOUR GOALS

You now know which shows meet your goals. However, before making a final decision, contact previous exhibitors and ask them the questions you asked the show manager. They will generally give you honest, straightforward answers. But don't rely on just one or two — you may get a biased opinion.

If you get a negative response, make sure that the fault was not with the exhibitor. When things go wrong, the show manager often gets blamed unfairly for things that were due to carelessness or lack of planning on the part of the exhibitor.

If you get a preponderance of negative comments, then be careful — ask the show manager what he or she is doing about the complaints. If the response isn't satisfactory, look elsewhere.

An ideal way to make a final check is to visit that show as a guest, rather than as an exhibitor. If the show is an annual show, this may be too long to wait for your current marketing plan and you will have to fall back on the opinions of others who have been to the show. As a second option, you may want to visit other shows run by the same management. This would give you first-hand experience of their management capabilities.

If you are able to visit a show before you exhibit, spend a couple of days there. Note the quality of the audience. Study their badges. Talk to other exhibitors. Study the booths and get a feel for what you will be competing with. Spend your two days observing everything about the show, keeping in mind your list of questions.

d. DECIDE HOW MUCH SPACE TO BOOK

The final decision, before taking the plunge, is deciding on the amount of space needed, which is tied directly to your goals.

The standard booth is usually 10 ft. x 10 ft. (approximately 3 m x 3 m), although this may vary from show to show. Space is priced either by the square foot or meter, or by booth according to location and size. Large islands and corner booths often carry a premium and many of the more desirable locations are booked year after year by the same companies. If you want one of these prime locations, you may have to wait until one becomes available.

1. How to determine your booth space

There are a number of factors that determine the size of booth you choose. What follows is a sample calculation based on goals set in the manner described in the previous chapter. Following the calculation is a detailed discussion of the six major variables that can affect your choice of booth size.

(a) Step 1

Use the following rule of thumb: A semi-private conversation with one salesperson and one or two prospects requires 50 square feet of booth space.

(b) Step 2

Calculate the number of hours during which you can expect good traffic at your booth. These are called active hours. Non-active hours are times when traffic is expected to be light.

In the previous chapter we discussed show patterns and how they were affected by such things as your location, special speakers, seminars, and social events. If you think that any of these factors will affect the traffic at your booth, then you should designate the times at which they occur as non-active hours.

Your chart of active hours might look like this:

Show hours		Total hours	Non-Active	Active
Sun.	9:00-6:00	9	2	7
Mon.	9:00-6:00	9	2	7
Tues.	9:00-6:00	9	2	7
Wed.	9:00-6:00	9	2	7
Thurs.	9:00-3:00	6	2	4
	Total Active Hours			32

(c) Step 3

Refer to your goals and calculate the number of sales-people you need on duty during the active hours.

Let's assume that your goal is to talk to 2,137 people during the show and to find from them a total of 427 good leads. Dividing the number of people you talk to by the number of active hours tells you how many people you must handle every hour. In this case, 2,137 divided by 32 gives almost 67 persons per hour.

If you assume that each salesperson can qualify 15 people each hour and reduce this figure by one-third to allow for presentations to qualified prospects, then you arrive at a figure of 10 persons per hour. This means that you will need 6.7 or 7 salespeople on duty to cope with the expected traffic.

(d) Step 4

Calculate the amount of booth space required using the rule of thumb outlined in Step 1. If you need 7 sales-people and 50 square feet per person, you will need 350 square feet. If a standard booth is 100 square feet, you will need 4 booths.

You will need to modify this calculation to take into account the variables discussed below.

2. Variables

These are the variables which you must consider when calculating your needed booth space:

(a) Your product

(b) Your traffic goals

(c) The image you wish to project

(d) Cost

(e) An existing exhibit

(f) Availability of space

(a) Product

If your product is a 50 ft. (15 m) conveyor, you'll need a booth at least 60 ft. (18 m) long. If you have a lot of small items arranged on display boards, then you'll need sufficient wall space to hang them in a pleasing and eye-catching manner. You also need space for literature and a small table. If you have four sales representatives on duty, then you need room for at least eight people to be in the booth at the same time without crowding.

In an average 10 ft. x 10 ft. (3 m x 3 m) booth, it is recommended that there be no more than 2 salespeople at a time. This number does not necessarily increase proportionately with the size of booth. Other factors such as the space taken up by your displays must be taken into account. For example, a 20 ft. x 40 ft. (6 m x 12 m) booth (equivalent to 8 standard booths), with a walk-through display, could well be staffed adequately with 8 to 10 people.

(b) Your traffic goals

The size of your booth must be directly related to the number of buyers you wish to contact during the show. If, as explained in chapter 1, you have determined from your demographic information that you expect your sales staff to talk to 12 to 15 people an hour and to get 5 leads per hour from them, then it is a matter of simple arithmetic to determine how many people you need on duty at a time.

The numbers also tell you that during the busiest period of the show, your booth has to accommodate 9 salespeople, plus visitors. It is not inconceivable that you could have 15 to 20 people in your booth at any one time. And if you want your share of visitors to walk through your booth and not straight by, then it must not look overcrowded or too busy to bother with.

The traffic you wish to handle is the most practical factor in determining booth size. To handle 15 to 20 people, a minimum of 400 sq. ft. (e.g., 40 ft. x 10 ft. or 20 ft. x 20 ft.) or 36 m^2 (12 m x 3 m or 6 m x 6 m) would be needed, again depending on the size of your displays. This calculation assumes that 50% of the booth area is taken up by your display and allows approximately 10 sq. ft. (1 m^2) per person including staff and visitors.

If, for other reasons, you can't have a booth this size, then you should revise your goals or look for another show that allows you to reach this goal.

(c) The image you wish to project

Creating an image can take several forms. If appearing to be bigger and better than the competition is your goal, then your booth size will be determined by what the competition does.

If you wish to be seen as the supplier of a new line of products, then you must take the space necessary to adequately display the products and their salient features.

When you want to be seen as the supplier of a wide range of products, then you need room to display at least a representative sample of those products backed up by adequate literature and catalogues.

(d) Cost

The cost of booth space is a small portion of the overall cost of exhibiting at a show. However, the size of your booth does affect the total cost in terms of staffing, travel, booth design, construction, and planning. Compromises are often necessary and this is where you'll find the ranking of your goals (as discussed in chapter 1) helpful.

(e) An existing exhibit

Displays can cost thousands of dollars to design and build and are often amortized over several fiscal years. Make sure your design is flexible enough to handle shows of different sizes.

(f) Available space

Shows often sell out and have a waiting list. Even booking early in a popular show is no guarantee of getting the space you want unless you have been a regular exhibitor. Show managers naturally give priority to previous exhibitors and often do not allocate space to new exhibitors until after a pre-set deadline has been reached. After this deadline, applications are usually treated on a first-come-first-served basis.

From what we've discussed, you will see that an early and close working relationship with the show management will provide answers to many of your questions and signal potential problems long before they become reality.

If the demographics are not in line with your goals, or other factors make it unlikely that your primary goals will be met, then you should not enter a show, even if your competition is there. Just make sure that your evaluation is accurate and unbiased and that you haven't missed something the competition has spotted. If you're sure of your facts, and convinced that your primary goals won't be met, then spend your money more effectively on other forms of marketing, or choose another show.

3

CONTROLLING THE COST

Since many of the costs involved in exhibiting are fixed well ahead of time, there is a tendency to bypass budgeting and allocate a lump sum for shows. The result is a seat-of-the-pants operation with very little recorded data to fall back on.

Shows should be treated as a profit center. Your show budget helps you focus your activities, keep your team on track, and give you the tools needed for your post-show evaluation (see chapter 16). What's more, with so many of the costs fixed, budgeting for a show is much less of a guessing game.

Preparing a budget allows you to work through the show on paper, with input from each team member, before committing any funds. This means your budget must be done early — in fact, as soon as you have set your goals and picked the right show.

Early budgeting has several advantages:

(a) It brings the overall program into sharp focus.

(b) You have tight control.

(c) You have time to adjust and make changes without incurring cost overruns.

(d) Services can be ordered well ahead of time, avoiding those rapidly escalating late charges.

To make the task a little easier, you can divide the budget into bite-size chunks, which are discussed in this chapter.

a. SPACE RENTAL

In addition to the cost of your booth space, space rental also includes hotel space for your staff, hospitality suites, and space for press conferences. You should be able to obtain firm prices for these items from show and hotel managements.

Show managers often designate one or more official hotels where blocks of rooms at special rates are made available to exhibitors. You should mention that you are exhibiting at the particular show, otherwise you may be told that the hotel is fully booked. Hotels often supply show managers with reservation forms for easy booking.

It can't be over emphasized that early booking is essential if you want to be where the action is. Late bookers often end up in out-of-the-way hotels, which means extra daily traveling and added costs.

b. DESIGN AND CONSTRUCTION

If you are constructing a brand new booth, you should include the cost of all materials and labor involved in designing, manufacturing, setting up, and equipping your booth. Don't overlook things like shelves, tables, carpets, etc., if these items are to be supplied by you. If you plan to rent some items, they should be budgeted under show services.

The full cost of a new booth is often amortized over several shows and only the pro-rated portion is included in the current budget. Where modifications are made to an existing exhibit, or repairs are required, the full cost is usually charged to the current budget.

You should also include in this section the cost of packing cases that will adequately protect your exhibit on its many journeys. If you are also planning to exhibit abroad, consult an expert on the best type of packing to use for overseas shipment.

c. TRANSPORTATION

You have the choice of using a common carrier or a mover who specializes in exhibit transportation.

A common carrier will pick up your goods and deliver them to the receiving area or specified storage area at the show. However, you have no control over how your goods travel from one point to another. If you are shipping from one large metropolitan area to another, your goods will likely be picked up by a local delivery truck, transferred to a large cross-country vehicle, and delivered at the other end by another local delivery truck.

If you have fragile or sensitive equipment, then the official carrier may be your best choice. In some cases, you will get direct door-to-door service with the same truck and crew. In other cases, the carrier may consolidate shipments locally, then ship them directly to the show to arrive at the time designated by the show manager.

Official carriers often arrange to consolidate foreign shipments at designated border points, collect the necessary documentation from the shippers, and clear them through customs.

Whichever method you choose, you should consult with your shipper early (make them part of your team), and get an accurate estimate of shipping costs.

One other cost that is sometimes borne by the exhibitor is drayage — that is, the movement of your goods within the exhibition hall. Ask the show manager who pays drayage, and if he or she says it is your responsibility, be sure to include it in your budget.

d. SHOW SERVICES

Show services include electrical, plumbing, janitorial, carpentry and security services, furniture rental, and the provision of signs, utilities, audio/visual equipment, photography, and telephones. The contractors who supply these services are often designated by the owners of the exhibition hall through long-term contracts. Neither you nor the show manager may have any choice in the matter. In other cases, some of the contractors may be designated by the show manager, while others may be left to your own choice.

Some services you pay for directly, others are included in the booth space charge. You must read the exhibitor manual carefully to find out what is supplied. Where contractors are designated, show management usually supplies order forms.

If you have doubts about any services, clear them with the show manager well ahead of time. Leaving service orders to the last minute can cost you a hefty premium and possible delays in obtaining what you need.

e. PERSONNEL

In order to get a true picture of your show participation you must account for the costs associated with the people involved. These costs are usually divided into two categories: direct and indirect.

Direct costs are those related to the show staff. These should include set-up crew, sales, administrative, and registration. In addition, there are those costs related to the booth staff, such as travel and living allowance.

Indirect costs are those for the support people who spend some time organizing and administering show activities. These include secretarial, clerical, and accounting staff.

f. ADVERTISING AND PROMOTION

The opportunities for advertising and promotion in connection with a show are endless. Trade and business publications often have special pre-show issues. Local radio, TV stations, newspapers, billboards, direct mail, and the show guide offer numerous promotion opportunities.

A discussion of show advertising and promotion can be found in chapter 5.

g. MISCELLANEOUS

This is a catch-all category for those one-time expenses you'll incur. Included are items such as speakers, entertainment, insurance, parking, show training, etc.

Worksheet #2 gives a detailed list of items for which you should budget. Notice that there is a second column for you to enter the actual costs and a third column to note the difference. This will be a valuable reference guide for budgeting future shows.

h. SOME TYPICAL EXHIBITION COSTS

In a 1988 research report (Cost Analysis #2060), the Center for Exhibition Industry Research, formerly the Trade Show Bureau, noted that the average expenditure for booth space for 248 exhibits in 55 shows over the period 1985 to 1987 represented 24% of the total direct cost dollars spent on the shows. In addition, 33% more was spent on salaries and travel expenses for exhibit personnel.

This means, on average, for every $100 spent on space rental, you can expect to spend a total of $554 on the show as a whole. Use this figure with caution since it is the average of a wide range of shows of varying complexity and size. The pie chart shown as Figure #1 is reproduced from this report.

In particular, amortized construction costs decreased by 26% in the latest report, while show services and transportation showed a combined increase of 52% over the same period.

Since individual shows vary so widely in size, market, and allocation of costs, it is difficult to give firm figures for budgeting purposes. However, many of the costs are readily available from show management and others who have participated in the same or similar shows in previous years.

If you are new to show business, talk to your show manager, other exhibitors, and everyone on your show team. If you keep good records, you'll soon have a valuable body of information and experience on which to base your future planning.

Figure #1
How the show dollar is spent

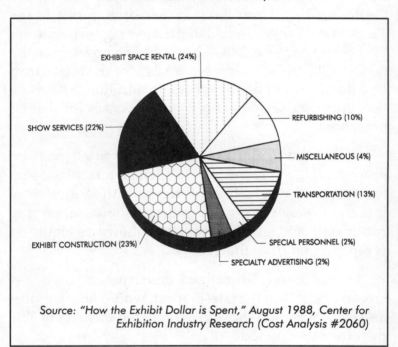

Source: *"How the Exhibit Dollar is Spent," August 1988, Center for Exhibition Industry Research (Cost Analysis #2060)*

Item	Budget $	Actual $	Difference (+) or (-)
1. Space rental			
Booth space			
Hospitality suite			
Hotel rooms			
2. Design & construction			
Booth design			
Construction			
Packing design			
Display materials			
Set-up/tear-down			
3. Transportation			
Freight			
Drayage			
Customs & brokerage			
4. Show services			
Electrical			
Plumbing			
Janitorial			
Security			

Item	Budget $	Actual $	Difference (+) or (-)
Utilities			
Telephone			
Equipment rental			
Furniture rental			
Other			
5. Personnel			
Staff salaries			
Temporary staff			
Meals & accommodation			
6. Advertising & promotion			
Print advertising			
Radio & TV			
Direct mail			
Catalogues			
Premiums			
7. Miscellaneous			

4

CREATING YOUR DISPLAY

Your booth must visually differentiate you from the competition and attract immediate attention. In one quick glance, attendees should be able to know who you are, what product or service you have, and what solutions you offer.

To a newcomer, booth design may seem a daunting task. However, a well-organized, step-by-step approach can help you quickly overcome your initial concerns and produce great looking, workable displays.

a. UNDERLYING PRINCIPLES

We can apply the same principles that govern advertising to the design of an exhibition booth. An advertisement has to capture readers' attention quickly before they turn to the next page and forget the message. Likewise, your booth has to capture attendees' attention before they walk to other exhibitor's booths. So, let us take a page out of the ad creator's book.

Recall one lifestyle advertisement that you regularly see on TV or in a magazine. The one you can recall quickly obviously got your attention. How? The story line may have been of a spectacular sports car being driven through breathtaking scenery, or of a family enjoying an exhilarating cross-country ski. Initially it may seem that the sports car or family trip had nothing to do with a product or service. The story was merely a device to capture your attention. Different storylines will appeal to different demographic groups. Now that your interest is piqued, you stay to listen as the story unfolds.

The messages will consist of a series of catchy phrases linking the scenes you have witnessed to the advertiser's product. What you now see may be seductive or appealing to your fantasies. If it is, the ad has created desire.

The final scene is a call to action. "Buy now!" or "Available at your nearest distributor" or " Call now, while supplies last." These statements all demand viewers to act.

Use the acronym AIDA to recall each of the four advertising principles; Attention, Interest, Desire, and Action.

Attract Attention

The sports car or family trip was carefully selected to attract the interest level of a certain demographic group. If the group of customers we are targeting changes, so does the scenario.

Build Interest

As the story unfolds, the viewer becomes increasingly engrossed in the action. This is accomplished with a tie-in that charges the viewers' emotions. It is a blatant effort to appeal to viewers' greed, envy, love, hate, anger, frustration, etc.

Create Desire

The catch phrases and visual links create a desire for the product. The underlying message is that this product will help you accomplish your goals. Using celebrity spokespersons is a common technique. "I could look like Cindy Crawford if I switched to Revlon," or "Jell-O must taste great if Bill Cosby says so."

Demand Action

A punch line that climaxes the drama demands viewers to act, with phrases such as "limited offer" or "Our operators are standing by" or "Join the Pepsi generation."

Follow these same guidelines when designing your booth. You must attract attention and build sufficient interest for your visitors to take you seriously. The connection between the signs, graphics, and booth hardware helps create a desire. This gets visitors out of the aisles and into your booth for your call to action.

That is Marketing 101. There is no universal answer to what makes one booth better than another. You cannot please everyone. You should be aware of tastes and aesthetic reactions from country to country, culture to culture, and person to person.

It might seem that the best booths are a result of the depth of the exhibitor's pocketbook. However, spending large sums of money does not guarantee a better booth.

Designing your booth is more than an artistic exercise. While there needs to be an element of artistry in the booth, it is the interpretation of the rules of exhibiting into an aesthetically pleasing three-dimensional display that presents booth builders with their greatest challenges. There has to be a careful balance between creativity and fiscal restraints. Creating the right booth is a matter of understanding some basic guidelines and finding ways to make each fit your situation. Follow these basic guidelines and your booth will contribute to your overall show success.

b. DETERMINE YOUR OBJECTIVE

In chapter 1, we defined your exhibiting objective in detail. Your focused objective will fall into one of two broad categories: sales or communication. Your objective is the nucleus for every decision you need to make. Your challenge is to find a three-dimensional display that will help you achieve your objective.

c. ESTABLISH A BUDGET

In chapter 3, you learned that 23% of the show budget was spent on exhibit construction and another 22% of the budget on show services. Take a detailed look at how that exhibit design dollar was spent.

Most of the exhibit budget expenditure was in new construction. This does not mean that every exhibitor needs a new booth for every show. However, it is a clear indication of the number of new booths that will be competing for attendees' attention. Your hardware, if not replaced, must be updated constantly. This means refurbishing should be an important part of your exhibit budget. By cleverly updating your exhibit, you will be presenting a fresh, eye-catching display each time.

Table #11
1996 Proportion of direct exhibit design dollar

New construction	65%
Refurbishment	25%
Rental	5%
Storage	3%
Design	2%

Source: CEIR, report SM22

Refurbishing need not be extensive. Small changes such as new furniture, signs, graphics, or product placement will do the trick. Fifty-one percent of all attendees want to see something new. If you want to attract their attention, show them something new.

d. *KEEP IT SIMPLE*

Some attendees complain that shows are a confusing place to do business. They spend hours on the show floor bombarded with information from dozens of booths, demonstrations, and eager booth staff. Coupled with this is the vast amount of information gleaned at show-related workshops and presentations.

It is no wonder that attendees eventually lose their focus. Too much information in your booth will add to their confusion. The solution is a clean, simple, yet powerful presentation that allows attendees to quickly know who you are and what you have to offer.

Simplicity is the key to a successful booth presentation. Many exhibitors typically complicate their booths with excess information, signs, graphics, demonstrations, give-away items, and a multitude of products and services often from more than one corporate division. Put yourself in the attendees' shoes and you begin to understand how bewildering a show can become.

The answer is to understand that your display does not have to tell the whole story; it has to get the attendees' attention. Your display is not a reproduction of your corporate brochure. When you are planning what goes into your booth, remember, less is better.

e. FIND A FOCAL POINT

To capture attendees' attention, you must give them a focus. A well-designed booth will include signs and graphics that provide an eye-catching focal point for the information-overloaded attendees.

Signs and graphics serve two purposes: to stop and grab the attention of people passing your booth, and to enhance the story you have to tell about your products and services.

The key to good signs and graphics is brevity. Following with the premise of simplicity, use bold and easily recognizable names and logos. To emphasize the main selling points of your products or services, stick to essential facts and present them in a quickly readable manner. Make one strong statement, rather than ten weak ones. If you can tell the story better with a picture, do so.

There are two types of signs and graphics that work in a show setting: showstoppers and informational.

1. Showstopper graphics and signs

(a) Showstopper graphics

A showstopper graphic is one attendees can focus on quickly. It is one large image on your back wall rather than several small ones. The image is what gets visitors' attention. Recently I attended a real estate show. One exhibitor had hung approximately 75 framed photographs of its current listings on the back wall. Clearly it had attempted to replicate the storefront of a real estate company, a story board that gave passersby a feeling about the types of listings this agency carried. This works well in a non-show environment, but at a show, the result was overloading information on those who are already information overloaded.

The solution here is simple. If the exhibitor had a clear idea of who their potential customer was, it could easily choose one listing that represented all the dreams and fantasies of that targeted customer. Whether the listing chosen was a fact or a fantasy, it does not matter. Design the showstopper graphic to get customers' attention. In this example, a blow-up of a villa overlooking the Mediterranean or a chalet in Aspen would work well. You want the attendees to walk by the booth and say "Wow!" Figures #2 and 3 are examples of two good showstoppers.

(b) Showstopper signs

Showstopper signs are those signs that tell attendees quickly who you are and why they should visit your booth. Avoid the tendency to over-word your booth with information that attendees cannot and will not take the time to read. Find one message that will give attendees a reason to stop.

Figure #2
The 5 Second Baby

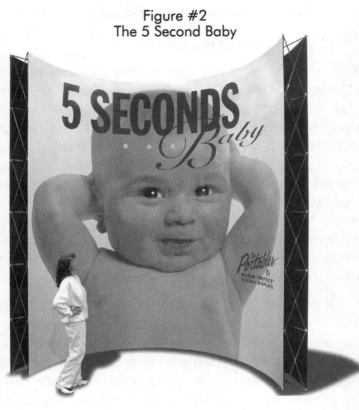

Courtesy of The Portables.

Your showstopper sign should contain no more than seven words (plus your business's name). It takes about three and a half seconds for visitors to walk by your booth. They simply do not have enough time to read a lot of copy.

By understanding what you are trying to convey to the attendees, you can develop your seven-word (or less) slogan. This slogan tells visitors how your products and services will help them. Watch good marketers as they develop snappy, to the point, short statements

Figure #3
Sumo Wrestler

Courtesy of Hanna Design/Scan.

that express why you should use their product or service. For example, the Mazda Miata is sheer "passion for the road."

2. Informational graphics and signs

(a) Informational graphics

Informational graphics help the booth staff make presentations: it is helpful during a presentation to have a picture or two that explains how things work. A picture is worth a thousand words, but use only enough pictures to help, not enough to confuse.

(b) Informational signs

It is the same with signs. One or two well-thought-out signs listing products or services or benefits can help reinforce a message to attendees. Use signs to point out new or interesting features of your products. Don't ignore the value of three-dimensional models with cutaway views or mirrors showing what is behind.

(c) Tips for good graphic design

Here are other pointers to good graphic design.

(a) *Corporate logos.* Don't overemphasize your corporate logo. Remember, the point is to convey information quickly to passersby. If your company's name is a household word, as many large consumer brand names are, make it as big as you like. Now, everyone will know what you are selling. If your business name isn't a household word, don't overpower the sign with the name. Rather, give equal emphasis to the message, balancing the two.

(b) *Letter size.* If the letters on your sign are too small, people will not be able to read them from a distance. If they are too large, they may overshadow any other message you are trying to deliver.

Figure #4, originally published in *The Exhibit Medium* by David Maxwell, sets out the relationship between letter size and the minimum distance at which a person with normal eyesight and under normal lighting conditions can see it clearly. The distance refers to how far away the reader is from the message. The letter size refers to readable size at those distances.

Figure #4
Signage

Feet	Distance Meters	Letter Size Inches	mm
10	3.05	$5/16$	7.9
20	6.1	$11/16$	17.5
30	9.1	$1 1/16$	27.0
40	12.2	$1 3/8$	34.9
50	15.2	$1 11/16$	42.9
60	18.3	2	50.8
70	21.3	$2 1/4$	57.15
80	24.4	$2 1/2$	63.5
90	27.4	$2 3/4$	69.9
100	30.5	3	76.2

Measure the depth of your booth and the width of the aisle to arrive at the maximum distance you must take into account when calculating letter size. The thickness of black lettering should be approximately one-fifth to one-sixth of the height.

f. ESTABLISH YOUR IDENTITY

A colleague of mine recently attended a show, looking for a client of his who was exhibiting. "This was a large recognizable company," he explained. "I walked the whole show and left frustrated because I could not find it."

It turned out that the client was there with a large, attractive exhibit. However, my colleague missed the booth. The problem stemmed from my colleague's familiarity with the company's national TV advertising: he had become familiar with the images. This company ignored all its other marketing, abandoning all the recognition developed by other marketing efforts, and took a completely different approach at the show. This caused confusion and therefore missed business opportunities.

Identity is more than a name. Your corporate identity was established long before the show. Since shows are one part of the marketing mix, they provide an opportunity to reinforce the messages the public is seeing, whether on TV or the radio or in print. Take advantage of the identity you have created and bring these elements into the booth.

g. ATTRACT ATTENTION

When polled, exhibitors noted that the top three elements to remember exhibits by were size of the booth, interest in the product, and a live demonstration.

We cannot always have as much space as we would like. It is not the wisest way to exhibit — it may leave too little resources for other exhibiting considerations. Let us see what happens to these numbers when we delete the effect of size.

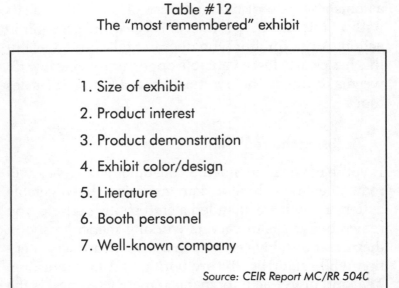

Table #12
The "most remembered" exhibit

1. Size of exhibit

2. Product interest

3. Product demonstration

4. Exhibit color/design

5. Literature

6. Booth personnel

7. Well-known company

Source: CEIR Report MC/RR 504C

Table #13
Top reasons other than size for
remembering an exhibit

Interest in products	39%
Live demonstrations	25%
Exhibit color/design	14%
Booth staff	10%
Obtained literature	8%
Well-known company	4%

Source: CEIR report MC/RR 504C

As you can see from the figures above, an astonishing 64% of memorability of an exhibit deals with an interest in a product or service and seeing it in action. Any exhibitor who does not take advantage of this has clearly lost a valuable opportunity. So, how do we make our demonstrations into a powerful sales tool?

1. Bring the real thing

If you have ever attended a consumer show, you will remember the exhibitor demonstrating the vegetable cutter. If you have attended a craft show, perhaps you remember artists or carvers working meticulously on their creations. Live activity in the booth attracts attention while static booths are boring and uninteresting. The kind of live activity that is remembered best is the kind that reflects the use of the product or service. Showing attendees the real thing in action is superior to showing it on pictures or graphics.

However, what happens if your product is too big or it is financially unfeasible to set up at each show? Simple. Create a working model. Alternatively, if your product is too small to be effective, blow it up into a larger version. If you have not piqued visitors' attention, they will not stop. This is "Show biz."

2. Show what it represents

Demonstrating the "real thing" is fine for tangibles. What does an exhibitor do with intangibles or when a working model does not present the right solution? The answer is to focus on what the service represents to customers. Let us look at the example of life insurance.

When purchasing a life insurance product, the tangible is nothing more than a contract — not a very stimulating thing to bring to a booth. Still, what we are really buying with life insurance are things such as security, peace of mind, and lifestyle. When you focus on what the product represents, you find clues to the kind of things that might attract visitors: retirees talking about their peace of mind, audiovisual demonstrations showing the benefits of protection to a family, or a booth designed as a comfortable home that will reflect a lifestyle dream. When you start to think about what the tangible represents, you can usually develop ways of showing your attendees your message.

Take another example: tourism. If you are in the tourism business and operate a lodge, hotel, or destination resort, bringing the "real thing" is obviously impractical, and creating a scale model might not provide the right impact. Step back and think about what makes your location special. What is your real message? What does your property represent to your customer and how does it differ from the competition?

If you have the world's best bass fishing lodge, bring the bass. If you are promoting a nature camp, bring the animals, a campfire, or burnt marshmallows. If you have a rock climbing club, bring backpackers climbing rocks. Let your creativity run wild.

3. Video

Video is another useful tool to use when you have a product or service that is difficult to demonstrate. There are two types of videos you could use: showstoppers and informational.

(a) Showstopper video

A showstopper is the video most often seen at shows. It is situated close to the aisle and attracts visitors' attention as they walk by. This video's purpose is to attract attention only, not to tell the whole story. Visitors will not stand around and watch a lengthy video. There are simply too many other things to see at the show and their feet are probably sore. For maximum impact, the video should be no longer than 90 seconds and formatted on a continuous loop.

Showstopper videos are placed at eye level with the sound set at a reasonable pitch: not too loud so that it interferes with other exhibitors and not too low so that it is completely inaudible.

One word of caution. Some shows have become over-videoed. At these shows you find many exhibitors with the same size monitors showing similar videos. Visitors quickly become desensitized and no longer pay attention. The wise exhibitor looks to larger screens, multi-screen presentations, or even three-dimensional presentations to create impact.

Videos vary in price depending on length and quality of production. However, a well-made video can be used often and its cost amortized over several shows. It may also be suitable as a field sales tool that will help justify the cost of production.

(b) Informational video

If you must tell your story in more detail, an informational video can form part of the presentation. These videos vary in length, often running as long as 15 minutes. A live presentation often accompanies them. You must have enough space for the audiovisual equipment and seating for the visitors. The presentation needs to be dynamic enough to keep visitors in their seats. Often exhibitors reward visitors with a gift for staying.

4. Multi-media

Shows have become a frenzy of touch-screen presentations, computers, Internet connections, virtual reality demonstrations, and interactive games. Technology is advancing faster than its applications. The world seems fascinated by new gizmos and technologies. The big advantage of multi-media is that it appeals to visitors and gets them involved. However, multi-media for its own sake is not enough. Choose to have a multi-media presentation only if it is the most effective way of demonstrating your products and services. There are limitless numbers of applications for multi-media presentations. Here are two tips for presentations.

(a) *Keep the interaction short.* Creating multi-media presentations that entice visitors into a long stay defeats your purpose. It creates line-ups and attracts those intrigued with the technology (rather than with your products or services). Whether you program your multi-media to tell a story or gather information, keep the interaction short — a minute or two should suffice.

(b) *Be able to operate the technology.* There is nothing more frustrating than high-tech equipment that is impossible to operate. Don't fall into the trap of "it's simple, everyone knows how to work these." We all have different levels of electronic sophistication. Some attendees will be patient

81

with your multi-media presentation and some will not. Don't count on your visitors to wait around while your equipment is being set up or fixed. Having booth staff who understand how the equipment works and are responsible for its ongoing maintenance is important.

h. PLAN TRAFFIC MANAGEMENT

Usually, open and inviting booths that encourage visitors to walk in and browse are more effective than those that constrict traffic flow. Your graphics, signage, products, and demonstrations will attract visitors, but before visitors will enter your booth space, they need to see a way to get into the booth easily. They also need to see a way out. The feeling of being trapped will turn off potential customers.

The easiest way to create good traffic flow is visualizing visitors walking through your booth. Is there a clear path for them to follow? Have you inhibited traffic flow by setting a table across the front of the booth? Notice if your products, furniture, and demonstrations are all placed properly and if your booth staff is creating an entry barrier.

i. BOOTH COMPONENTS

1. Lighting

When properly and professional done, lighting can give your booth mood, highlight important areas, and attract visitors. Proper lighting can make your booth a pleasant and inviting place to work. Skimped on and improperly placed, lighting can make your booth hot and uninviting and will have a negative affect on the people working in the booth. It can cause strained eyes, a leading contributor to headaches and short tempers.

In the past, lighting was a secondary booth consideration. However, exhibitors have become aware of the advantages of a well-lit booth. The general rule is that despite the quality of light in the exhibit hall, each exhibitor needs individual booth lighting. Well-thought-out booth lighting will attract visitors' visual attention and direct their eyes to specific areas of the booth.

You can create a mood with spots, floods, or colored lights, depending on the effect you want. By adding brilliant lighting, you can make a boring booth dazzling. Halogen lights are very popular because of their reduced power consumption. One 600-Watt halogen bulb can adequately light a 10 ft. x 10 ft. (3 m x 3 m) booth. Halogens produce a warm white light and a bright image. The disadvantage is that halogen will change colors, particularly of food and skin tones, so check first.

If the exhibit hall is conducive, and the show rules allow, hanging overhead lights is often a good alternative. They flood the booth with light while remaining unobtrusive.

The use of a valance with a ceiling in the booth and indirect lighting behind is becoming more popular. It allows the eye to focus on specific areas of the booth and again remains unobtrusive.

When placing lights, look for shadows and blind spots, and adjust accordingly. You may want to try suspended or indirect lighting to create the desired effect. All electrical wires and outlets should be hidden for safety and aesthetics.

A dry run before you ship the booth to the show gives you time to work out any design or lighting problems.

2. Color

Color is generally more attractive in booths than black and white. However, there are some examples of the use of black and white that are very dynamic. As you walk through various shows, you are sure to come across black-and-white graphics with one color emphasizing a product, service, or message. The yellow pages advertising with a splash of yellow in a black-and-white print advertisement, which you may have seen in your local newspaper, is a good example.

Color will help you develop mood and atmosphere. If chosen properly, color will show your products and services at their best. But picking the right color can be difficult. There are countless variables as you become an international exhibitor. Culture and taste will play an important role in your decision. The general rule is to consider culture and taste and then choose a color that will complement your products or services.

Seeing how people equate color to specific preconceived messages is interesting.

We equate many emotions with color. We "see red" when we are angry and are "green" when we are envious. Blue signifies coolness and black is morbid. Colors may have different meanings in other cultures. White, for example, has always been synonymous with purity or virginity, and consequently, is in North America a popular color for wedding dresses. Yet in Japan, white is the color used at funerals. In Brazil, purple is the color of death. And in India, red or yellow is used at weddings.

In Sweden, green is associated with cosmetics or toiletries, while in Malaysia, green is associated with disease. In North America, green is associated with environmentally friendly products and services.

In England, red is considered old and out of date, but in Japan, the combination of red and white is associated with happy occasions.

By ignoring cultural interpretations of color, you could inadvertently create a booth that repels visitors rather than one that is an attractive and appealing place to conduct business.

Color is an integral part of the overall display. Most exhibit builders agree that your primary source of color in the booth should come from graphics rather than back walls. Dynamic graphics will give your booth "eye appeal" while the colors you choose for the furniture and back walls should be neutral or complimentary. Try to coordinate the back wall color with your other booth components such as the carpet. This is particularly important for those exhibitors who choose to rent accessories when the choice of matching colors may be limited.

If you have a corporate color, make sure it does not distract visitors' attention away from your products and services. Bright colors such as red and yellow are naturally attractive, as are greens and blues for outdoor themes. Earth tones might be used for food themes, white for winter scenes. Don't use colors such as black or purple which have morbid overtones. Avoid setting signs against backgrounds that make the copy difficult or impossible to read.

Use a color wheel, a tool used by interior designers, to select colors that work with one another. Color wheels are available at art supply stores or the booth designer may have one. Each element of the mix can complement or work against the other, so careful consideration of all items is necessary.

3. Storage space

Your booth is your temporary office and must be set up to conduct business. In your plans, allow space for things such as stationery, literature, lead cards, business cards, samples, and an extra pair of shoes. By planning for these things ahead of time, you can create space that includes cupboards and drawers that does not inhibit the attractiveness of the booth. Make sure your staff understands the importance of keeping items such as staplers, pens, premiums, tape, coats, and briefcases in their designated space. Odd items left lying around look sloppy and unprofessional.

4. Carpets

Carpets add to the aesthetics of your booth and help reduce fatigue. If you own your own carpet, make sure it is secured with doublesided tape. If you rent, the installer will look after this. Don't use carpets with open loops; high heels are apt to get caught. If you cannot find good quality carpet, install a thick underpad.

Carpets should be cleaned every day, either by your staff or by janitorial services. If you own your own carpet, it should be professionally cleaned every two to three shows.

5. Plants and flowers

Plants and flowers give your booth a warm and inviting look. A flower arrangement or potted plant can give the booth a look of completion. It is a subtle message to visitors that you have taken care of every detail.

Positioning is important. Make sure plants and flowers do not interfere with traffic flow or obscure part of your display. Under hot lights, flowers need constant care to survive. If you choose artificial plants, make sure they are of good quality.

6. Telephones

If you need a telephone, make sure it does not distract from the overall look of your booth. Telephones are for keeping in touch with your office, using the line to connect to the Internet or fax, accessing help lines, or placing clients' orders. Telephones can be useful in your booth as long as they are not abused. Booth staff should understand the real purpose of the telephone and keep away from it as much as possible. The temptation to make a call is always there, but remember, you and your staff must always focus your attention on the visitors.

j. SHIPPING CONTAINERS

The shipping containers are designed and manufactured along with your booth. Remember that since their primary purpose is to protect your display against damage, you cannot afford to skimp. Think of your shipping containers as pieces of luggage. If the booth is part of a permanent display, it will never be moved and you do not need the luggage. If you are going to move it only occasionally, you can afford a less expensive piece of luggage. But the more you move your booth and the farther away you take it, the more important is the issue of shipping.

A secondary consideration is ease of handling. Typically, small exhibitors want booths they can put into the trunks of their cars or vans. Larger exhibitors often have specialized staff to handle the booth details.

There are four broad groups among the variety of packing cases that you see at a show.

1. Custom-designed self-contained booth

A custom-designed self-contained booth is a self-pack unit in which the shipping crate is also the booth. When opened, the crate becomes a freestanding booth or part of the booth.

2. Custom-designed individual packing crates

Custom-designed individual packing crates made specifically for your booth are generally for larger exhibits, and the packs can also hold furniture. One common problem with this type is their weight. Not only is there extra shipping and drayage charges but once the crate is placed in your booth before assembling, moving it can be a chore. Wheels on the case can solve this problem. You should prominently label the crates inside showing the location of all components and the proper packing procedure.

3. Prefabricated packing cases

Prefabricated packing cases come in a series of standard sizes. Inserts hold your products and prevent movement inside the case. These cases are often made of molded plastic, and store easily.

4. Systems packing cases

Each system manufacturer offers packing cases custom designed to hold their systems. Often these are made of molded polyethylene, which is a bit more expensive than other materials commonly used in making packing cases, such as wood or plastic, but it is very durable. When you buy one of these systems, you have the option (highly recommended) of buying the packing case(s).

All packing cases should have adequate systems of labeling and numbering for both forward and return shipments.

k. SHIPPING AND DRAYAGE

Most show organizers appoint an official shipping company. It is worth checking out. This company's rates are usually competitive because it can consolidate large loads at its major terminals. The official shipper will also notify you of the required pick-up date to ensure that your materials arrive on time. At the show, the official shipper often gets priority in unloading and access to drayage.

If you are shipping offshore, it is best to meet in advance with the shipper you have chosen to work out details, including customs and brokerage. The show manager often includes forms for this purpose in the official exhibitor's guide. Make sure you understand what the quoted shipping costs cover. Often these costs do not include the cost of drayage, that is, the cost of moving your materials from the loading dock to your booth location and, after the show is over, back to the loading dock. Drayage is sometimes included in your booth rental fee; other times it is an extra charge based on an hourly fee or weight. If you are in doubt, check with your show manager.

I. SET-UP

1. Planning

Planning the set-up of your booth is a crucial step on the road to success. Your exhibit must be ready and looking its best when the show opens. Attend to all last-minute details. Nothing looks more lonely than an exhibitor with an empty display, waiting for products to arrive.

You have many choices that will ensure the proper set-up of your booth. You can use the official show contractor whose name you will find listed in the show guide, you can use an independent contractor, you can do it yourself, or you can use a combination of any of these options.

Before deciding, check with the show manager to make sure there are no restrictions. For example, in some exhibit halls, collective agreements may prohibit certain activities from being carried out by non-union representatives. By ignoring these limitations, you may cause delays. So be sure to check and plan accordingly.

Another consideration is your familiarity with the venue. If you are exhibiting internationally and are not familiar with local rules and regulations, you may be unaware of certain exhibiting techniques. This is why many first-time exhibitors use their governments to help them in show planning. Through trade missions and other programs, governments sometimes make booths available at important international trade fairs to first-time exhibitors. Government officials are usually available to help take care of the many problems that may arise, including the supervision of the set-up and tear-down of booths.

2. Timing

All shows have specified times for exhibitors to unload their materials and set up their booths. You must respect and be ready to work within these times.

By arriving at the last minute and scrambling to get your booth ready on time, you are leaving yourself little time for last-minute changes and corrections. If you need extra services such as electrical or the furniture you have ordered has not been installed, you may find yourself at the end of a long line of exhibitors, all anxiously demanding service.

By arriving at the last minute, you add to the stress of working in an unfamiliar environment. You need all of your high-level energy for working the show. Remember Murphy's Law: Anything that can go wrong, will go wrong. Do yourself a favor and get to the show in good time and save yourself extra hassles.

Plan to arrive at least one day before the show opens and, if there is sufficient move-in time, ask for your booth to be installed and ready before you arrive. Check the dates and times in the exhibitor's guide, and give yourself enough time to set up properly, solve last minute problems, and start the show on a positive note.

3. Show services

Whether you use the show contractor to set up your booth or do it yourself, there may be times when you will need help and advice from the official contractors. Some exhibitors spend a few hours at the show before the set-up, meeting with the show contractors and familiarizing themselves with the facilities. This could be time well spent — remember Murphy!

When contracts govern the services, book your time well in advance to ensure you get what you want, when you want it. Contractors will provide order forms in the exhibitor's guide. These forms usually have a firm deadline, after which the charges for the service offered may be increased.

If you use an independent contractor, your contract should be specific and include the complete set-up and tear-down of your booth with a time schedule for each phase of the contract. If the exhibition hall is unionized, specify that the independent contractor is responsible for dealing with the union contractors if required.

Where services are concerned, do not assume anything. There are many different contractors at the site who perform specific functions (e.g., carpenters, electricians, picture hangers, floral displayers, photographers, etc.) Unions, if involved, jealously guard these functions. Read your exhibitor's guide carefully. Otherwise, you may jeopardize your exhibit and even the show.

4. Rentals

You might want to rent a display rather than purchasing one. There are many rental options, from a simple backdrop to a more elaborate display. You can rent virtually every component. Renting is an excellent option for the first-time exhibitor or those exhibitors who want to offset some of their shipping and set-up costs. Check all your options with your show services contractor.

Display houses also offer rentals. Give them plenty of notice to ensure that the right components are available when you need them.

5. Equipment and supplies

The supply and installation of special equipment needs to be carefully thought-out. Special equipment includes audiovisual equipment, signs, lights, computers, demonstrations, games, storage for samples, water, refrigeration, and compressed air.

You must first ensure that your plans do not conflict with any of the show rules. Once you have confirmed that your plans are acceptable, you can attend to the details. Here is a list of things to check.

(a) Electrical: current and voltage requirements and availability, outlets, adaptors, extensions, and whether approval of electrical equipment is required (CSA, ASA, hydro, etc.)

(b) Video format: VHS, Beta, PAL, etc.

(c) Restrictions: signage, booth height, floor loads, lighting, running water, and gas use

(d) Regulations: fireproofing

(e) Amount and location of storage for perishables and non-perishables

(f) Regulations if gambling or prizes are involved with booth games

(g) Rules covering shipping and receiving during the show

(h) Adequate quantities of office supplies such as business cards, order forms, premiums, and brochures

(i) Additional security or material handling, if needed, that goes beyond that provided by show management

A tool kit to cope with last-minute show needs is also a good idea. Checklist #1 lists items you should include, but include anything else you think you might need.

m. TEAR-DOWN

Once the show is over and the last visitor has left the hall, a scene of frenetic activity erupts. Exhibitors and contractors will be scurrying around trying to be the first out of the building. Your inclination may be to do the same; however, it's worth your while to take your time and tear-down properly.

Ask the show manager where your packing materials are stored and when they will be available. While tear-down usually begins once the show closes, it may be some time before your packing crates arrive at the booth. If they have been stored behind other packing materials, you may

Checklist #1
Tool kit checklist

- ☐ saw
- ☐ hammer
- ☐ screwdriver
- ☐ pliers
- ☐ nails screws
- ☐ nuts and bolts
- ☐ washers
- ☐ wire
- ☐ rope
- ☐ ruler
- ☐ flashlight
- ☐ caulking
- ☐ adhesives
- ☐ knife
- ☐ light bulbs
- ☐ extension cords
- ☐ scissors
- ☐ picture hooks
- ☐ touch-up paint
- ☐ carpet tape
- ☐ lint brush
- ☐ marking pens
- ☐ pencils
- ☐ aspirin

be among the last to receive yours, so plan accordingly. You must allow yourself adequate time. If your show closes at 4 p.m., don't book a flight home for 6 p.m. If possible, wait until the next day to leave.

While guards or show management staff will be posted at the doors, security in the hall is minimal once tear-down starts. Unless you take steps to secure your valuables, they can easily disappear in the rush. Once easily pilfered items are secured, pack all display items just as carefully as you did when shipping them out.

When they are packed, you can take down the booth. Be careful to avoid damage that may make it difficult to assemble next time.

Pack the booth carefully in its crate, following instructions to make sure each piece goes into its appointed place. Label each box with the labels supplied by your shipper and which you have filled out beforehand. Arrange for drayage and return all your shipping documents to the shipper's agent, who usually has a desk on the show floor.

Now you can go home and start filling orders or following up on your leads.

n. THE EXHIBIT BUILDER — A CONSUMER'S GUIDE TO PICKING THE RIGHT ONE

Choosing an exhibit builder can be a daunting task. A renewed interest in exhibiting has fuelled the growth of a competitive design industry. Display builders boast of their sure-fire solutions. Differentiating the various products and finding the right display builder for you is hard work.

Some exhibitors use the yellow pages. Another method is to create your own pre-qualified list of display builders. Visiting shows is a good way to find exhibit builders and to see their work in action. As you walk the aisles, pay attention to exhibitors who have products and services similar to your own. Notice the detailed workings of their booth. Stand back and watch how show traffic responds. See booth people work with clients and note if the booth helps or hinders presentations.

When you see a booth you like, and you have observed it in action, approach the exhibitor and ask for the name of its builder. If the exhibitor has time, talk to him or her about the booth. Now you have your first qualified display builder for follow-up.

Repeat this exercise as often as you think necessary. There are a variety of booths and a vast array of services from which to choose. You will want to consider several builders and do some comparative shopping, so take your time.

On your first look around a show, you will probably see a bewildering array of different booth designs. Closer examination will show that most booths fall into two broad categories: system and custom.

1. System versus custom booths

Traditionally, system products were generally hardware oriented while custom booths focused more on the image the exhibitor wished to project. However, a lot has changed in the industry.

System booths are mass-produced units with interchangeable parts. They boast portability, flexibility, and adjustability. In the past, portability was one of the strongest selling features. Each structure is designed to fit into convenient carrying cases that are easy to transport.

New construction methods and the creative use of materials have also added the element of flexibility. With good planning, most system booths can take on a customized look that in the past was another strong reason to choose a customized booth.

The third element is adjustability. Most systems are adjustable to a variety of shapes. By adding or subtracting components, the exhibitor can create in-line, corner, peninsula, island, and L-shape booths.

Custom booths are different in that every component is entirely under your control. Each part of the booth is created to your specific needs. The result is often a design that reflects the exact message you are trying to convey. The disadvantage is that custom booths are bulkier to handle and take more time to assemble and tear down. As you talk to exhibitors, question them on how they use their booths and the booths' pros and the cons. It should quickly become apparent whether you need a customized or a system booth.

There are many different types of systems on the market, each with its claim to portability, ease of set-up and tear-down, and flexibility in customizing to your own requirements. While many systems lend themselves to customization and allow you to show your individuality, often the systems element is still recognizable. If you want something unique, a custom booth is the answer. Bear in mind that although there may not be an appreciable difference in the purchase price, there is a difference in shipping, drayage, assembly, and tear-down costs.

As you continue your search you will quickly expand the definition of the two basic kinds of booths into four generic types. Look at all four and decide which will work best for you. At some shows you will need a full booth, at others a "table-top" will suffice. Both are available in the four generic types described below.

Understanding the four types will help you focus your search for a booth builder.

2. Portable pop-up

While many system makers like to call their structures portable, the really portable booths can be assembled and disassembled in minutes. They can often be taken on an airplane as baggage. Most portable designs are back-wall displays only. With clever graphics they can be eye appealing and show a positive image. Although the initial cost may be higher, the cost-saving factors

Figure #5
Portable Pop-up

Safari. Photo courtesy of Hanna Designs.

such as shipping and drayage should be considered. Flexibility is limited with this booth. What you see is what you get. Figure #5 shows a portable pop-up booth.

3. Modular

A modular system (see Figure #6) is an arrangement of preconstructed modules fitted together to form an eye-catching display. When choosing a modular display, you should note the following characteristics.

(a) Sturdy construction with interchangeable parts

(b) Ease of assembly and tear-down with a minimum of tools

Figure #6
Modular

NEC. Photo courtesy of Nimlok Canada.

(c) Good choice of shapes and sizes

With these characteristics, you can have a system that will serve you for many shows. The different sizes and shapes allow considerable flexibility in changing your look from show to show. When well constructed, the pieces fit properly and require little maintenance.

The drawback to this type of booth is the growing number of components. As your needs change, there is a tendency to add to your basic structure (this is both good and bad news). The more you add, the bulkier it becomes.

Figure #7
Custom

*Designed and fabricated by Sparks Exhibits for adidas America
1997 NSCAA Annual Convention.*

4. Custom

A custom booth (see Figure #7) is one that is designed with a particular look in mind. Its focus is on the image rather than on the hardware. The biggest advantage to a custom booth is that it will say exactly what you want.

Although the cost of purchasing a custom booth is comparable to some systems, shipping, drayage, storage, and labor are often higher. Some labor-saving techniques can be incorporated into your booth with the use of Roto Locks or plain nuts and bolts.

5. Structural

Purchasing a structural booth (see Figure #8) is analogous to buying a meccano set. The booth is a series of

Figure #8
Structural

Courtesy of Alphaform Exhibits and Design Inc.

102

panels, connectors, pipes, and lights that when magically erected offer you a sophisticated structure. However, they can be a challenge to assemble. On one hand, structural booths offer total flexibility. Their disadvantage is the cost of assembling and tear-down, which can be extensive because of the large number of interchangeable parts.

6. Booth rental

Most large exhibit houses have rental services. For the first-time exhibitor, this may be a good option. It gives you a chance to see what works best for you before you buy. Often the show will appoint a service contractor to provide rental booths at the show. There are many rental options, from a simple backdrop to a more elaborate display. Virtually every component of your booth can be rented. Figure #9 shows a rental booth.

7. Choosing an exhibit builder

Once you have decided which type of booth best meets your needs, and you have a number of references, you are ready start shopping. If you live in a large metropolitan center, chances are many exhibit builders will have local offices. If they don't, call the builders for information on their local representatives. Alternatively, it might be worth your while to take a trip to a larger center and line up two or three appointments.

Your first meeting with the builder should be exploratory — a chance to find out whether you can work with each other. Set out the ground rules carefully. Go prepared to gather information and give the exhibit builder the details the builder needs. Take a few minutes

Figure #9
Rental

Althon. Photo courtesy of Freeman Decorating.

to complete Checklist #2. Supplying the builder before your meeting with the information you have compiled by using this checklist will give the exhibit builder enough information to be able to answer your questions properly.

By completing Checklist #2 and presenting the same information to each exhibit builder, you will be able to compare "apples to apples." As you interview each exhibit builder, you will find some who are clearly not suitable for you while others will be on your shortlist.

Checklist #2
Exhibit builder's checklist

1. Background
☐ *Service or product*: A brief description of the products, service, or programs you want to bring to a show.

☐ *Objectives*: What are your measurable and quantifiable exhibiting objectives?

☐ *List the shows which you are planning to attend*: Names, dates, location of your future exhibits

☐ *Amount of space booked in each show*: Total square feet (or meters)

2. Previous show experiences
☐ What worked/what didn't?

☐ Why was it good or bad?

☐ Last year's show (bring pictures)

3. Special requirements
☐ Budget

☐ Current market tie-ins

☐ Art work: existing or new?

☐ Corporate information: color, logos, etc.

☐ Lighting

☐ Amount of product

☐ Other media you are now using

☐ Audio/visual requirements

☐ Copies of current literature

☐ Weight: products, displays, etc.

☐ Theme

☐ Multi-media

☐ Furniture

☐ Carpet

☐ Literature racks

☐ Samples

☐ Demonstrations

☐ Premiums

☐ Your business's logo

Once you have narrowed your choices to a shortlist of no more than two or three, ask for more detailed drawings of each builder's proposal. Offering to pay for this work gives you the flexibility of buying parts of your booth from other suppliers. The cost of these drawings may run from $250 to $1,000. If you take this approach, let the booth builders know what your plans are.

With drawings in hand and your checklist complete, you are now able to choose the right exhibit builder. One final word: do not ignore the importance of chemistry. Having an exhibit builder who meets all your criteria is useless unless you feel comfortable enough with the builder to talk openly and freely. There must be a certain level of comfort between you and the people with whom you are dealing. If your relationship with the exhibit builder is good, the builder will be forthcoming with suggestions. If it is strained, you may be running the risk of dealing with people who are prepared only to tell you what they think you want to hear in order to get the sale.

Choosing your exhibit builder should be completed early, at least three months before the show. This will avoid last minute panics, and costly errors and changes.

8. Design schedule

Once you have selected an exhibit builder to design and manufacture your booth, set up a realistic schedule for its completion. Allowing at least three months for the booth to be built will give you time for reviews of the working drawings, artwork, videos, and any other components.

Table #14
Your 90-day schedule

Day 1 – 10: create the initial design

Day 11 – 30: design revisions

Day 31 – 73: booth construction

Day 74 – 81: booth set up and last minute revisions

Day 82 – 90: ship to the show and assemble

9. Operation and maintenance

You have taken great care in selecting the right booth and its accessories. You must also take care to ensure that it is kept in top shape. Here are a few rules to follow to extend the life of your booth.

- Adjust and clean your booth regularly

- Store your graphics properly: flat and in a controlled climate

- Check booth structure once a year

- Refurbish annually — changing the look of your booth will help attract traffic

Graphics have a one-year life span because you should be changing the look of the booth every year.

Don't go back to the same show without some sort of change.

Hardware (walls, attachments, lights, etc.) has a five-year life, depending on the number of shows. If an exhibitor does six to seven shows per year, five years is a reasonable life expectancy for the booth. After five years, it will need to be refurbished or traded in.

You have now taken care of one important element toward your overall show success — a great-looking booth. However, doing a show and having no one show up is a waste of time. To ensure you get your share of visitors, you need a good promotional plan. We'll discuss this in the next chapter.

5

PROMOTING YOUR EXHIBIT

As we saw in the previous chapter, promotion plays a large role in the success of any show and requires the active participation of both show management and exhibitors. You can maximize the effectiveness of your own promotional efforts by making them complementary to those of the show manager, as well as other exhibitors.

Many exhibitors rely completely on the mailings and advertising carried out by the show manager as their only source of show promotion. In a study carried out by the Center for Exhibition Industry Research, formerly the Trade Show Bureau, the impact of direct mail pieces sent by show organizers was analyzed. They found that only 17% of the potential audience remembered the mailing piece as their reason for attending the show.

While show management may use much more than mail, it should be clear to the exhibitor that the goal of the show manager, through all their pre-show promotion, is to attract as many qualified people as possible to the show. On the other hand, your pre-promotion goal is to attract people who meet their qualification criteria to your booth.

This does not mean that the show organizer's promotional efforts will not help individual exhibitors, but it is a clear indication that you cannot rely solely on its promotional efforts. As an exhibitor your needs are unique; at best the show manager can be a great help in giving the show the right profile and image, but attracting the right people to your booth is up to you. Don't blame the show manager for poor promotion if you've done little to promote your own participation.

In a 1982 study for the Center for Exhibition Industry Research, Robert T. Wheeler identified eight factors that influenced visitors to trade shows:

(a) *Obligation* was the most important influence for 25% of respondents. They regarded visiting the booth of an existing supplier as "an obligation of past business activities."

(b) *Habit* was the second most important reason quoted by 23% of respondents. They looked forward to visiting regular exhibitors every year.

(c) *Personal invitation* was third with a 15% response, underlining the value of extending personal invitations immediately before the show.

(d) *Trade journal publicity* came next with 12% of the respondents who reacted to advertisements or editorial copy in a trade journal.

(e) *Other advertising* brought in another 9%. This includes radio, TV, billboards, other magazines, etc.

(f) *Mail invitations* or other promotional literature sent by mail also resulted in a 9% response.

(g) *Recommendations* from associates were listed by 4% of the respondents.

(h) *Not sure* was given by the remaining 3%.

The first two categories in this list account for almost half the visitors to a booth, emphasizing the importance of letting your customers and prospects know where you are and what new products you have to excite them this year.

Although statistics are not available for consumer shows, it is reasonable to assume that similar considerations motivate people at these shows. How many times have you said, "Let's go and see what 'so-and-so' has on display this year"? Habit and familiarity with suppliers and their products are always good drawing cards — if you dangle the carrot of exciting new things to see. People soon tire of seeing the same things year after year.

Planning your show promotion activities can be divided into three broad categories: pre-show, at the show, at the booth.

Each category should be regarded as a stepping stone to the next, and none should be neglected. Each activity should be a well-orchestrated event with every facet planned and coordinated to complement your other activities so that the whole comes together as a professional and highly successful presentation of your products or services.

a. PRE-SHOW PROMOTION

Your objective here is to let as many prospects and customers as possible know that you are participating in the show, where you will be located, and why they should make sure they visit your booth. You should generate some excitement and expectations by describing briefly

111

new products, features, or benefits — and don't disappoint them when they show up.

The various means of promotion are discussed in detail below. Remember to try and dovetail them into the show manager's promotion plans so that they complement one another.

1. Direct mail

For existing customers, direct mail should be designed to reinforce their feeling of obligation to visit your booth.

For prospects you can use mailing houses, publishers, and list brokers. If available, you can pick names from the list of last year's attendees provided by the show manager.

Whichever lists you use, always direct your promotion to a specific person by name. Direct mail that is not addressed to a person more often than not gets "junked." If your list is missing some names, then it's worth the time and effort to phone the company and find out the name of the person to whom you should address show information.

Your direct mail pieces can take many forms. They need only be in the form of a short letter or a simple printed card containing your name, booth number, and a compelling reason for your prospect to visit your booth. Reasons quoted could be the introduction of a new product or service, a chance to meet and talk with a product expert, or the offer of a special gift.

2. Telemarketing

As the results of the survey quoted above show, as many as 15% of your visitors are influenced by personal invitations. Telemarketing is one of the best means of conveying personal invitations, provided it is done professionally.

Your telemarketing script should be carefully planned and prepared. It should be targeted to the person receiving the call. This may mean preparing several different scripts — one for manufacturers, another for wholesalers, and a third one for retailers. Each script should outline the benefits of your product or service to the person being called, and it should be phrased in such a way that the person's interest is gained very quickly.

The script should also request some form of response from the prospect, such as:

"Good morning Ms. Jones, I understand you're attending the industry show on behalf of your company, is that correct?"...."Great! While you're there I would like to extend an invitation to visit ABC company's display in booth 303. You'll see something there I know you'll find very exciting. It's sold over a million pieces in a related market and our studies show that it has similar potential in your market. Can you tell me which day you plan to attend...?"

When you list the one or two benefits that relate most strongly to your prospect, you should phrase them in a manner that will arouse their curiosity as in the example above. Benefits can include show specials, give-aways, or special product introductions. Use the benefit that will appeal to the person you are calling.

In some markets, you may have to be very specific, so make sure that your telemarketer has all the necessary information readily available.

3. Appointments

Some people prefer to make appointments to see specific exhibitors in order to avoid the crowds and waiting that inevitably go with a busy show. Appointments can be made by your representatives in the field or by your telemarketer. In the telephone conversation in the previous section, after the prospect had indicated on which day she planned to attend the show, the telemarketer could have continued like this:

"Good. Tuesday, as you know, is a very busy day at the show and we're expecting loads of people. If we can make an appointment for a specific time, I will make sure that one of our representatives will be available to demonstrate this exciting new product and save you having to wait around. What time will be better for you, morning or afternoon?"

4. Magazines and business papers

Most shows have several magazines or special interest publications that cover the fields of interest of attendees. This interest is fostered by advertisements and editorials that are specifically targeted to their field and is supported by detailed demographic data available from the publisher.

Many publishers prepare special pre-show editions of their publications that are often bumper issues. This allows the publisher to give in-depth coverage of the show in the form of detailed listings of the exhibitors and products. These editions are usually distributed shortly before the show and help visitors locate the booths they wish to see and plan their visit beforehand.

Because of the high profile accorded by the editorial coverage of the show, many exhibitors prepare special advertisements for these pre-show issues, often highlighting their exhibit and always inviting the visitor to see them at their booth.

If you have something new or special, contact the editors of the magazines and offer them information on the product for inclusion in their pre-show issue.

The editor may ask you to write it up and send it in, or a staff member may be sent to your office to get the story first-hand. Many editors send out letters soliciting information for these special issues. This is an opportunity you should make the most of. Editors welcome well-written, factual copy supported by professional photographs. If it fits the editorial profile of their publication, they'll most likely use it, so study the style of each publication before you prepare anything.

Some trade magazines also publish daily issues during the show highlighting special events, late-breaking news about products and exhibitors, vignettes of prominent exhibits and many other promotion opportunities for a publicity-conscious exhibitor. Talk to the editor of your favorite trade magazine and find out what the magazine plans to do at the show. These show dailies often carry advertising at special show rates and can help boost your image at the show.

5. Press releases and press kits

Press releases and press kits are powerful promotional tools that can get you publicity that would otherwise cost thousands of dollars to buy.

Your press release must be sent to the various editors in time to meet their publication deadlines. Check beforehand to determine the proper dates.

At your show, make sure copies of your press release are placed in the media room. Most shows have a room set aside for the press which is usually staffed by a person whose job is to help the press cover the show.

Releases can vary in size from single-page announcements to elaborate multi-page presentations in attractive folders. Choose whatever you feel the occasion demands (and your budget supports). Here are some basic rules that should be followed in the preparation of these important promotional tools.

(a) If you haven't anything really worthwhile to say, don't say it! Editors are busy people. They get hundreds of press releases each week. They want solid information for their readers and anything in the nature of a "puff" heads straight for the round file. Even worse, anything you submit in future probably won't rate more than a glance. So, review whatever you write dispassionately, or better still, get a colleague who isn't as involved in the product as you to review your release and tell you whether it's worthwhile.

(b) Remember "KISS" (keep it short, stupid). Long rambling releases don't get read. Make your opening sentence a real grabber to get the editor's attention.

(c) Every press release should have a first page (it may be the only page) that contains the following:

  (i) Company name, address, contact name, phone and facsimile numbers.

  (ii) Title of release, date and city of issue, name of company official making the announcement, name and date of show.

  (iii) Brief description of product, its importance, features, comparison with current products, benefits and market at which it is targeted.

  (iv) Availability, delivery, and price.

  (v) Brief description of company, its products, and market.

  (vi) List your booth numbers at the show.

(d) Establish a working relationship with the editors of the publications that are most important to you. Find out from them how they like to receive material, what their current editorial requirements are, when their deadlines are, and what color and size of photographs they prefer.

(e) Don't assume that because you're an advertiser you'll get preferential editorial treatment. Many editors resent this kind of pressure. If you have a product that is of interest to the readers (and you should if you're an advertiser), and it is presented in a factual, professional manner, then it may be used whether you are an advertiser or not.

(f) Always address the release to a specific person. If you don't have a name, then take the time to get one. A phone call should suffice, or a look at the masthead of the publication. Some publications have a number of editors and it is important that you get the right one. Otherwise your release may get sidetracked and not reach the right editor until an important deadline has passed.

(g) You'll need a media list, and it must be properly targeted. There's no point in sending a release about a new gardening product to a lawyer's newspaper. But you can be sure that publications catering to homeowners, lifestyles, real estate, or similar topics will be at least prepared to read your offering. Make up your media list carefully, and constantly review it to make sure it is accurate and up-to-date. Make sure you know the deadlines of all publications on your media list.

(h) Avoid excessive claims and eschew the use of advertising slogans in your copy. Your release should be as matter of fact and straightforward as possible, while presenting your product, exhibit, or news announcement in a positive and enthusiastic manner. Above all, avoid "editorializing." (e.g., "Customers are unanimous in declaring our product as the most sensational on the market.")

118

6. Cooperative advertising

There are many opportunities for cooperative advertising that have the advantages of lower cost to you for a share of more prominent advertisements. They range from a manufacturer sharing space with distributors, to groups such as association members or government trade missions.

7. Pre-registrations and quality attendance programs

Show managers often run programs designed to stimulate quality attendance. These might include V.I.P. passes or pre-registration forms that can be mailed in ahead of time and often earn the visitor a discount if received by a specified date. While the show manager is responsible for organizing these programs, exhibitor participation is often encouraged. Free passes may be available or are earned in return for specified services. Check with your show manager.

If you need to be convinced of the value of pre-registrations, stand near the main entrance of your show when it opens on the first day. You will see line-ups of people who have filled out registration cards patiently — and sometimes not so patiently — waiting to get their badges typed. Once they reach the head of the line, have their information checked and pay their fee, they are shepherded to another line to wait for their badge to appear from a machine. In a busy show, as much as an hour can be wasted in this process.

Take a look at the booth in the reception area labelled "Pre-registered Guests." Here an attendee can go up to the receptionist and say, "Hi, I'm John Doe, I have been pre-registered." In a matter of seconds the badge is produced and the visitor can go into the show and start spending money.

Now, wouldn't that be a great service to offer your clients and prospects? Even better, some show managers mail the badges to the pre-registrants before the show so that they can go straight in without waiting at all. If you choose to be involved in one of these programs, don't forget to tell your clients. In the maze of show planning detail, little things like this can be easily overlooked.

8. Other materials

Show managers often provide other materials, sometimes free of charge, that you can use. These include stickers to place on your stationery, mailers, and invitations to special events. Another attention-getter is to revise the heading on your fax message form to include an invitation to visit your booth. You should take advantage of these offers as part of your pre-show promotion.

b. PROMOTION AT THE SHOW

You'll find several opportunities to reinforce your pre-show promotions while the show is on, both inside and outside the exhibition hall. They should help remind those you have already contacted to visit your booth and attract others who were missed by your pre-show promotions.

1. The show guide

Every visitor gets a show guide, which makes it an excellent vehicle for advertising. The listings of exhibitors and their products are usually free.

Advertising is sold by the publisher of the show guide. This may be the show manager or some other company, such as a publication house, which has contracted to do the job. Some show guides also carry short features on the more interesting new products. Once again, it pays to be in contact with the editor.

2. Press room

Many shows have a press room that is available to you for interviews with journalists. Copies of your press kit should also be available in the press room. Since there will be dozens of other companies' kits laid out alongside yours, an attractive, eye-catching folder will help make yours stand out among the crowd.

3. Seminars

A good program of seminars will help attract many visitors to a show who otherwise may not come. For exhibitors who sponsor seminars, it helps raise their profile, gives them an opportunity to focus on certain products, techniques, and applications in detail to a large group, and gives them the chance to invite more people to visit their booth after the seminar. If you sponsor a seminar, make sure that you have a good speaker who knows the subject well and can answer questions convincingly.

4. New product displays

Show managers sometimes set up displays of new and interesting products including "Best of Show" awards. They are often placed in areas of the show where show management wants to build traffic. The displays are usually well promoted and can be a valuable source of extra promotion for you. If you take advantage of this offer, be sure to include your company name and booth number in the display.

5. Billboards

These are seen outside the building, in the parking lots, and at approaches to the exhibition halls. In these situations they will be seen by a large number of the visitors to the show.

6. On-site hospitality and hospitality suites

At some shows, hospitality at the booth is not only appropriate but expected. The range of hospitality runs from light snacks and refreshments to wines and hors d'oeuvres. In many European and Pacific Rim countries, at-the-booth hospitality is expected. The extent of your at-the-booth hospitality should be geared to the type of show and the practices set by other exhibitors. For the first-time exhibitor, it is important to check out what's appropriate beforehand so that you can make adequate preparations.

Food and refreshments are for your guests, not for you. As tempting as they may appear, stay away. Of course, in some countries it is considered rude not to join in a drink or cocktail. If you do, remember that the show is long and your performance will suffer notice-ably if you indulge with everyone who comes along.

Many companies like to put on special events or reserve a separate area for their hospitality. The event could be as simple as setting up a hospitality suite in a hotel or conference room with food and drinks for the guests. Large companies may rent major facilities or host a major industry event featuring a high-profile, keynote speaker. The trick to making these investments pay off is to get the right people to attend.

For most small- to medium-sized companies, hospi-tality suites can be expensive. Your promotional dollars are often better spent on some of the other activities outlined in this chapter. If you have specific clients who you wish to entertain, you would be better taking them out to dinner. This will give you the opportunity to strengthen your business relationship on a one-to-one basis.

Major corporations and governments with their large personnel and management resources, as well as considerable clout in the industry, are the exhibitors who usually succeed with their hospitality suites. The important thing is to clearly state the goal of the event, such as prospecting, image building, entertaining exist-ing customers, attracting new customers, and so on. This will keep the staff at the event focused on what's expected of them.

Before setting up a hospitality suite, it's wise to check with the show manager. Some shows have rules that prohibit the use of hospitality suites during show hours.

The success of a hospitality suite depends very much on the people who run it. You should try to create a warm, friendly atmosphere where customers and prospects can relax and quietly talk about your products or services. You should have product information and knowledgeable people available to answer questions.

For the manager organizing a hospitality event, here's a checklist of the things you'll need to look after:

- Rent facility

- Order food and beverages

- Schedule host services

- Arrange decorations, displays, coat check, and security

- Book entertainment

- Organize news conferences

- Invite guest speakers

- Coordinate transportation

- Distribute invitations, tickets, and other correspondence

- Purchase gifts

7. Event sponsorship

Extra publicity for your exhibit can be obtained by sponsoring a special event during the show. This could range from a pre-show reception, a coffee break, seminar, or an evening event. Check with your show manager well before the show to see what opportunities are open for sponsorship.

8. Other ideas

Some other forms of promotion include the use of theme characters to hand out invitations or buttons, robots that wander the aisles, advertising in show dailies, handouts in participating hotels, bulletin boards to post notices for agents, reps, etc. Before you plan any of these forms of promotion, check with management to see if what you have in mind is allowed. Most shows have strict rules covering these other activities and it's wise to check before you spend any time or money.

c. *PROMOTION AT THE BOOTH*

Once visitors have found your booth, you must do something to keep them there for awhile. While not all of your visitors will qualify for a full presentation, many of them will be potential future customers and you want to make sure they remember you.

1. Premiums

The best way to make a lasting impression is with your personal sales approach that is discussed in chapters 8 through 11. Memories, however, are short, so it is a good idea to give visitors something tangible such as a pen, letter opener, etc., that will remind them of you in the days and months ahead. Here are some guidelines for using such premiums:

(a) Always print your company name and phone number on the premium. If it doesn't lend itself to an imprint, then it's not a good premium.

(b) The premium should tie in to your product somehow. Car dealers give away key chains because you need a key to start your car. If you can't find something, then put a short sales message on a pen or luggage label.

(c) Don't lay them out in dishes or piles for anyone to pick up. That gives the premium little value in the eyes of the visitor. Only give them out to people who show interest in your products. You could say something like:

"Thank you for visiting our booth. As a new customer, we would like you to accept this token of our appreciation."

By restricting the availability of the premium and tying it into a specific interest in your products, you have given the premium value in the eyes of the customer who is more likely to appreciate the gift and remember your company.

Picking a premium that is useful and at the same time ties in to your product or service can be difficult. If you do find a new and useful premium, it won't be long before others are copying your idea. The challenge is to stay ahead of the pack by being constantly on the lookout for new and exciting things to give away.

For example, the person who first thought of giving away plastic bags imprinted with their logo or sales slogan had a great idea. Unfortunately, so many exhibitors have copied this idea that its value has been greatly diluted. So, exhibitors must look for something with more impact.

One clever solution I came across at a recent show was an oversize shopping bag, printed with the exhibitor's name and logo, (and identified as being made from environmentally friendly materials). When a visitor came to their booth carrying several smaller bags from other exhibitors, they would approach them with an oversized bag and say, "Here, let me make carrying all that information easier for you." They would then take all the visitor's material and place it inside their bag.

2. Demonstrations and samples

Visitors come to shows to see, hear, feel, taste, and smell things. They are looking for a complete sensory experience of products and services. All it takes is a little creativity and imagination to adapt your exhibit to a live demonstration.

Choose your demonstrator carefully. Demonstrators should be knowledgeable, articulate, able to think on their feet, comfortable talking to crowds, and able to project a favorable image of your company.

After the demonstration, if it makes sense, you can give samples to those who stopped to listen. If samples are not practical, hand out a suitable premium.

With some imagination any product or service can be demonstrated. There are three ingredients to a successful demonstration: fun, creativity, and KISS (keep it simple, stupid). Your objective should be to bring some activity to your booth that will be both informative and entertaining.

Static booths do not draw the same kind of attention that booths with activity do — just walk around your show and see where the crowds go. Exhibitors who sell vegetable slicers, household gimmicks, or car chamois know the value of a good demonstration. Just watch the crowds gather around their booths.

A demonstration that shows your product or service in action is best. This means bringing the real thing to the show, whenever possible. However, if this isn't possible, bring something that shows what your product or service represents.

Insurance companies might have a hard time attracting visitors if they brought copies of life insurance contracts to the show. But, they know what insurance represents — security, safety, etc. So you'll see their booths filled with family pictures, or a scale model of a house with the lights on and smoke coming out of the chimney.

For some industries the demonstration could take the form of a game or contest. One imaginative mutual fund company put paper money in a transparent cylinder, kept in motion with a fan. The game was to guess how much money was in the cylinder.

Videos are widely used and can be a good answer to the company whose products are difficult to demonstrate live at a show. While this can be an effective method, some shows have too many videos and visitors quickly lose interest. If you find yourself in a show where every other booth seems to have a video, then perhaps you should come up with something more dramatic, like multi-screen presentations, or interactive video, or even three-dimensional video. Once again, it's a matter of trying to stay ahead of the pack; remember this is show biz.

3. Literature and price lists

Specification sheets, catalogues, brochures, and price lists should be treated in the same manner as premiums.

If you give them out to everyone, or lay them out for anybody to pick up, most of them will end up in the garbage.

A much better method is to mark a few copies in bold, bright letters:

BOOTH COPY
Please do not remove

Place these copies strategically throughout your booth. Have a few spares in your briefcase for immediate needs. When people show interest you can offer to mail them a copy after the show. If you promise to mail a copy to your qualified visitors, then it gives you a firm lead and reason to follow up.

4. Special events

Some shows stage special events at well-advertised times. These may take the form of a fashion show, a stage show, demonstrations, etc. By participating in these events, you can draw attention to your own booth or products.

One toy manufacturer, I recall, had a line of juggling products. He staged a series of juggling demonstrations that created a lot of interest.

5. Celebrities

High-profile people such as movie stars, athletes, politicians, business leaders, magicians, clowns, and local heroes have drawing power and can bring crowds to your booth. They can sign autographs, speak, entertain, or demonstrate. Whatever they do, make sure that the times of their appearances are well publicized and that the local media is invited. You might also want to arrange a press conference for the radio, TV, and press to interview the celebrity. Make sure that your company name and product is mentioned in all presentations and press conferences.

Among the crowds you attract will be a lot of curiosity seekers. Be on the lookout for those who show some interest in your products and be prepared to approach them as soon as the celebrity is finished. Construct a good opening line, as discussed in chapter 10, and begin the process of qualifying the prospect.

6. Models

Attractive models can have a positive effect on your exhibit if there is some reason for them to be there. I once saw a model sitting on top of a display case. She was there to make the point that the case was strong enough to withstand her weight. She was well dressed and able to answer customers' questions.

In many other cases where scantily clad models are used for the "cheesecake" effect, that's generally all the visitor remembers. Ask what the product demonstrated was, and in most cases he or she won't remember! Models should not detract from the product or service being shown but should complement it.

7. Contests

Before embarking on a contest, you should carefully review your goals for the show in relation to the contest. You should also review current laws at federal and local levels that regulate the staging of contests and make sure that what you propose is strictly legal.

If your goal is to collect new names for your mailing list and you are satisfied that the expected audience meets your broad criteria, then any sort of contest where the visitor is encouraged to place his or her business card or name into a box can produce the desired results.

One of the common complaints I hear from exhibitors about contests is the number of entries they receive from people who are not qualified. This presents a serious problem; if you don't contact all who entered, you run the risk of missing some real prospects. One solution is to pre-qualify those who enter the contest ahead of time. An easy way to do this is to force people to talk to you before they put their ballot in the drum. Design your ballot to ask the prospect for some basic information that will help to qualify the person as a prospect using the methods described in chapter 11. At the bottom of the ballot add a line which reads, "Must be verified by a booth person before depositing in drum."

Draws and contests can be an effective promotion tool only if they relate to your product or service and the entrants have a greater interest than just winning the prize.

A few years ago a community college decided to run such a contest with the purpose of gathering names of prospective students. The prospects would later be contacted by phone and asked to enroll.

The first time the college offered a TV set as first prize. Over 3,000 names were entered. When the entrants were contacted, the most common response was, "I just entered to win the TV."

On their second try, the college offered a $500 scholarship. The number of entrants decreased dramatically, but the number of enrollments showed a marked increase.

But, be careful; many show visitors become blasé about ballot boxes. I was at a show recently where I put a business card into the "Official Ballot Box," as it was clearly marked. A colleague asked me what the prize was and, to my surprise, there was no mention of any prize, yet the box was full. Draws obviously work, but you should take some of the steps mentioned here to get the most out of them.

8. Cross-promotion opportunities

By working with other exhibitors, there may be opportunities to cross-promote your presence in the show. The easiest example is to find another exhibitor who has a product or service that could be used in conjunction with yours. By loaning samples to each other for display, you effectively cross-promote each other's product. An example might be a manufacturer of computer furniture arranging to cross-promote with a manufacturer of computer hardware. The furniture manufacturer could display a computer system on his furniture with a sign saying, "Computers compliments of ABC at booth #123." Similarly, a hardware manufacturer could put out a sign which said, "Furniture compliments of DEF at booth #256."

Be on the look out for opportunities like this. They don't cost money and they are effective.

9. Public relations firms

How much of this kind of public relations activity should the average exhibitor expect to carry out on their own? Large corporations with in-house public relations departments will usually choose to assign a staff person to the task. Smaller companies can also do an effective job, providing they have someone on staff who has the time and interest to devote to the job, and some flair for communications.

Very often, however, an exhibitor will wish to rely on a public relations agency to handle the task. Ideally, the exhibitor has a P.R. agency regularly on call, so they do not need to explain the business of the firm or the nature of the products that are being exhibited. If not, a major show may afford the opportunity to bring in a firm, let them work one assignment, and then possibly establish an ongoing relationship for other work.

When looking for a P.R. firm, you have to look for the "right fit." A large multi-national firm will have little interest in a small client, while an enthusiastic freelancer may not have the back-up and support needed to do an intensive job over a short period of time. You should seek a firm with personnel who have some knowledge of your industry, and which can demonstrate successful past experience working with the media and handling show publicity. You may agree to pay a flat fee or an hourly rate. If you agree on hourly compensation, however, you should set a definite budget which you are not prepared to exceed. Finally the "chemistry" must be right: you and your public relations firm should be able to quickly develop a rapport and go about the task of effectively promoting your company.

Whether you do it yourself or hire a P.R. firm, you should work to a plan which sets out your goals, target publics, and the activities you will initiate over a period of a few months leading up to the show, as well as detailing what you'll do at the show.

We have covered a wide variety of promotional activities. Not all of them will be applicable to your business. However, it cannot be emphasized too strongly that your success as an exhibitor can be considerably enhanced with a well-planned and coordinated promotional plan that is designed to help achieve the goals you have set for the show.

6

YOUR RELATIONSHIP WITH THE SHOW MANAGER

Ask an exhibitor what he or she thinks of show managers and you'll get as many different answers as people you ask. Attitudes range from those who find show managers very helpful and cooperative to those who view them with a skepticism that almost amounts to hostility. Some even suggest that show managers take your money and, in return, do as little as they can get away with. Nothing could be farther from the truth in the majority of cases. Show managers are hard-working professionals who spend many hours planning, promoting, organizing, and running the shows with the long-term success of both the exhibitors and the show uppermost in their minds.

Smart exhibitors regard show managers as members of their show team and use them to the fullest extent possible. If the show doesn't work out as you expected, the first thing you should do is review your own activities, not blame the show manager for putting on (as you think) a poorly planned and promoted show. If a large number of exhibitors think it was a bad show, then they are probably right, but, generally, the problem lies with the exhibitor's failure to make the most of the opportunities offered.

In researching this book, a survey of show managers was conducted to examine the importance of the relationship between managers and exhibitors. Following is an overview of the survey.

a. *DO YOU PROVIDE A DEMOGRAPHIC BREAKDOWN OF PRIOR YEARS' ATTENDANCE?*

YES: 80% NO: 20%

Those who said no were consumer show managers: they said that a specific demographic breakdown of their attendees was not possible. One manager said that demographic information was provided only on request.

b. *DO EXHIBITORS ASK FOR MORE MARKETING INFORMATION THAN YOU PROVIDE?*

YES: 24% NO: 76%

Even though the majority said no, that doesn't mean they don't have information available. Often, the amount of information published is limited by the space available in their brochures. Some show managers conduct very sophisticated market surveys and use them as a guide to planning and promoting their shows. As an exhibitor, this detailed market information is often readily available if you ask for it.

As has been stressed many times in this book, shows are an important part of your marketing mix, and the more information you ask for, the better able you will be to make good marketing decisions. So, go ahead and challenge your show manager; ask for the information you need to make those important decisions. Even if all the information you need is not available, your questions will alert the show manager to issues to be researched for future shows.

Here is some of the information that show managers are asked for:

(a) Credit reports on every attendee

(b) Information on visitor's income levels

(c) List of delegates who will attend

(d) Whether visitors are from urban or rural locales

(e) Regional breakdown of attendees

(f) Occupational and industry breakdown of attendees

(g) Up-to-date market data

(h) A list of the other exhibitors who are showing

c. DO POTENTIAL EXHIBITORS DISCUSS THEIR SHOW OBJECTIVES WITH YOU?

YES: 55% NO: 28% SOMETIMES: 17%

One of the respondents said that he only discussed show objectives when asked to do so by the exhibitor. In a supplementary question, show managers were asked:

d. IF EXHIBITOR'S OBJECTIVES ARE NOT REALISTIC, WHAT ADVICE DO YOU OFFER?

I want to encourage you to open a dialogue with your show manager and the answers given to this question indicate that show managers are quite willing to work with potential exhibitors. It is in their interest, as well as yours, to make sure that your objectives are realistic. Many show managers commented on exhibitors promotional techniques and said that they offer guidelines, promotional literature, and information packages for exhibitors to distribute to their target markets. Here are more of their responses:

(a) Present guidelines of what they can expect from the show.

(b) Tell them how many contacts they should make in relation to the booth size.

(c) Try to help exhibitors target their objectives and focus on appropriate goals.

(d) Discuss the purpose of the event.

(e) Review show lead generating systems.

(f) Send printed material on how to set objectives.

(g) Coach them on staff training.

(h) Suggest they visit the show first.

(i) Give them names of other exhibitors in similar businesses to talk to.

(j) Assess their rationale for choosing this show.

Several show managers said that they would not hesitate to tell a potential exhibitor to consider a different show if they thought that the one they were considering would not give the expected results.

e. HAVE YOU EVER TOLD A POTENTIAL EXHIBITOR THAT YOUR SHOW IS NOT FOR THEM?

YES: 93%   NO: 7%

Professional show managers are concerned with the long-term viability of their show and do not like to see exhibitors in one year drop out the next. So it comes as no surprise that 93% said they would recommend that an exhibitor consider a different show. Here are some of the reasons given for making such a recommendation:

(a) Products not right for the show

(b) Audience not complementary

(c) In a juried show, rejected for quality of product

(d) Failure to meet rules and regulations (e.g., a distributor not a manufacturer)

(e) Trade exhibitors looking for consumer traffic

(f) Wrong image

(g) Exhibitor not experienced enough to meet standards of major show

(h) Product not related to theme of show

f. *DO EXHIBITORS COME TO YOU FOR OTHER EXHIBITING ADVICE?*

YES: 79%   NO: 14%
SOMETIMES: 3.5%   RARELY: 3.5%

The answers given to this question revealed a wide range of concerns on the part of exhibitors. Fortunately, show managers are well equipped to deal with most of these concerns — all you have to do is ask. Here's a list of the concerns expressed:

(a) Should they participate in this show, or are there alternative shows they should consider?

(b) How can they work effectively with the show manager?

(c) What size booth should they order and what is the best location?

(d) Advice on signage, booth layout, height of partitions, booth decoration

(e) Advice on pre-show promotion

(f) How to set a theme; how to attract people to the booth; recommended display houses

(g) Marketing and sales tips; number of people required to staff booth

(h) Shipping information; premiums; show specials

(i) Tracking leads; post-show follow-up

(j) Industry information

For most of these questions, the show manager can give you direct information or steer you to the right sources. However, this list is not exhaustive: show managers have a lot more information at their disposal as the answers to the next question will show.

g. WHAT WOULD YOU LIKE EXHIBITORS TO ASK YOU ABOUT?

Some of the following responses have already been reviewed, but they are well worth repeating. Here are the things that show managers would most like you to ask them about:

(a) How to set realistic show objectives

(b) How to judge if theirs is the right show

(c) Detailed marketing information

(d) How to work with show management for increased success for their own exhibit and the show as a whole

(e) How best to promote their own participation in the show

(f) The do's and don'ts of exhibiting

(g) How to work their booth effectively

(h) Which exhibitor support services are available

(i) Evaluation of results based on quality rather than quantity

(j) How to follow up leads

h. IN YOUR OPINION, WHAT DO EXHIBITORS EXPECT FROM SHOW MANAGEMENT?

The responses to this question suggest that some exhibitors expect show managers to be almost God-like in their abilities. Most exhibitors do not look upon show managers as partners in their enterprise but as someone who can solve their problems. Some of the responses received make sense while others suggest that exhibitors are asking for far too much from show managers.

Here's a list of reasonable demands:

(a) Good administration

(b) First-rate service during the show

(c) Personal consultations

(d) Regular communication of show changes

(e) Quick resolution of show problems

(f) Easy move-in and move-out

(g) On-site support and honesty

And here's a list of unrealistic expectations:

(a) Flexibility in the application of show rules

(b) Delivering the required audience without assistance from the exhibitor

(c) Quality leads

(d) Profits

(e) Do all the promotion

(f) Control the weather

i. WHAT DO YOU THINK EXHIBITORS SHOULD EXPECT FROM SHOW MANAGEMENT?

Show managers want to be your partner in your show activities, but not be held responsible when the failure is due to your own lack of effort or understanding of what's required to make a show successful. Here's what show managers think you should reasonably expect from them:

(a) You should feel that you have a partnership with the show management with ready accessibility to the manager's expertise and regular communication of information and accurate statistics

(b) Business should be conducted with courtesy, in a pleasant atmosphere, and with fairness

(c) The show should be held in a well-secured and clean building

(d) Efficient management, competent show suppliers

(e) Accurate, daily attendance statistics

(f) Encouragement and advice; positive suggestions for improved presentations; a sounding board

(g) A realistic return on show investment

(h) Make sure that it is the right show for exhibitor's market

Bear in mind that show managers are not there to solve all of your problems. Their function is to run an efficient and well-promoted show and to give advice and assistance when requested. They are not responsible for the success or failure of your exhibit. As has been stressed throughout this book, it is up to you, the exhibitor, to ensure that your exhibit is a success. The show manager's job is to provide the environment in which it is possible for you to be successful — if you do the right things.

j. WHAT PERCENTAGE OF EXHIBITORS DO YOU ESTIMATE READ THE OFFICIAL EXHIBITOR'S GUIDE?

Of the responses received, 15% had no idea at all of how many exhibitors read the guide. Of the remaining 85%, the answers were evenly spread between a low of 20% and a high of 70%, suggesting that there is little consensus on this question. From my own experience, when I ask at the open workshops I conduct how many read the exhibitor's guide from cover to cover, a figure of 4% to 5% is high, suggesting that managers overestimate the number of exhibitors that read this important document. The exhibitor's guide is an important document, and if exhibitors read it properly, many last-minute problems at shows could be avoided.

A successful show requires that rules, once set, have *no* exceptions; it is vital to have rules that every exhibitor abides by. Remember, some of those rules are forced on the show manager by local authorities such as fire departments and insurance companies. Don't blame the show manager for rules beyond his or her control, and don't try to get around them — you'll only find yourself paying double-time for labor to correct the deficiencies after the inspector has made his or her final rounds before the show opens.

k. WHAT HAVE YOU DONE TO ENCOURAGE MORE EXHIBITORS TO READ THE GUIDE?

Knowing how important the guide is in trying to avoid many of the last-minute problems referred to above, show managers have tried many different approaches to try and get more of their exhibitors to read and understand the guide. Here are some of the things they have done:

(a) Keeping it simple and as well organized as possible

(b) Using color-coded dividers

(c) Employing periodic reminders of actions to be taken; warnings of cut-off dates

(d) Printing special bulletins and separate order forms for critical activities which force the exhibitor to read the manual

(e) Using checklists and memos highlighting changes from previous show

(f) Personally delivering the guide to first-time exhibitors with first-hand explanation of how it works and its importance

(g) Holding meetings of exhibitors to explain requirements and answer questions

(h) Enforcing surcharges for late orders

(i) Offering prizes (draws) for those answering before deadlines

I. WHAT ADVICE DO YOU OFFER EXHIBITORS WHO DO NOT MEET THEIR OBJECTIVES AT YOUR SHOW?

Show managers' advice to those who do not meet their show objectives boils down to reviewing what you did in relation to your objectives and trying to analyze the reasons for failure. In many cases their advice follows the suggestions found in this book. Many recommend attending seminars on how to exhibit at a show. Here is a list of the things show managers would advise you to do if you experience disappointing results:

(a) Re-evaluate your objectives: Were they reasonable and realistic? Did your actions support your objectives? Was your staff aware of your objectives and sales techniques?

(b) Check your organization: Was your handout material clear and concise? Did your booth encourage active participation? Were contacts qualified at the show?

(c) Think about promotion: Did you promote your show participation effectively? How did your pre-show advertising and publicity compare to your competitors? Look at examples of what successful exhibitors did and what promotion they undertook.

(d) Hold a post-show meeting with your staff to evaluate what you did and why it wasn't successful.

146

(e) Evaluate follow-up procedures. Use buyers' lists to contact companies that didn't show up and set up appointments to see them.

(f) Ask if this was the right show, or if you need one or two more shows to get your name established as a supplier.

(g) Review staff training — perhaps they need to attend seminars on exhibiting and boothmanship.

m. ANY FURTHER COMMENTS?

In summary, it seems that show managers want to play a more active role in your show activities. They appreciate both positive and negative feedback from exhibitors. They have the expertise to guide and advise, but cannot be expected to solve all your problems. There is a clear need for more dialogue and for realistic expectations on both sides. Show managers also suggest the use of advisory committees made up of exhibitors to help develop good relationships between exhibitors and show management.

n. A FINAL COMMENT ON SHOW MANAGERS

One of your considerations when choosing a show should be the reputation of the show manager. Not all show managers are the same, and with the rapid growth in the number of shows over the past decade, it is inevitable that some less professional and inexperienced show staff have been attracted to the field.

If the show is being run by people who have as their main concern the long-term interests of their show and who have a proven track record in helping exhibitors, then you can be confident that they will run a good show. Show managers do not take your money and disappear for a year, as some people think. Planning and producing a successful show takes many months of hard work. It's up to you to choose your show and its management carefully.

7

INTERNATIONAL EXHIBITING

Exhibiting internationally presents both challenges and opportunities. However, to do full justice to this subject would require several volumes. This chapter gives you a broad overview of the highlights and key considerations that will help you ask the right questions before venturing into foreign markets. Do not think that you can venture into overseas markets and behave in the same way that you do at home. It won't work. You must study the local cultures of the markets you intend to enter and behave accordingly.

This chapter looks at three key areas of the world: Europe; the Pacific Rim; and Latin America (including Mexico and South America). Much of the discussion on cultural mores are generalizations and not meant to be stereotypes. Use them as guidelines only and do your own research.

Much of the material you have read in this book so far is North American in origin. The pizzazz and excitement that you have been encouraged to create in your booth is what North American audiences look for. Your assertiveness and personal style of approaching visitors is commonplace and quite acceptable to a North American audience. But don't expect everything to work at an international show. You must make adjustments to your exhibit and to your personal style.

One of the challenges you face as an international exhibitor is to learn as much as you can about the cultural and business norms of the country you plan to visit. Many of the pitfalls can be avoided if you do your homework. Remember, it's the little things that count and can often mean the difference between success and failure.

a. AN OVERVIEW

Historically, trade shows have not been the primary method of promoting products in Latin America, but they are starting to grow in popularity. The U.S.A./Canada/Mexico free trade negotiations have brought about a noticeable change in Mexico where North American attitudes to doing business are being adopted. It is expected that trade shows will play a significant role in doing business there in the future.

In Asia Pacific, trade and consumer shows are the fastest and most efficient way of entering these markets. A push for new, government-sponsored facilities is under way in this region, the most active areas being Taiwan, Hong Kong, Korea, and Singapore. These four regions boast more than 700 shows annually, and that number is growing rapidly.

In Europe, trade shows are as old as the hills. Europeans accept shows as a standard way of doing business and play host to some of the largest international trade and consumer shows in the world. Many of the larger shows run on two- or three-year cycles and attract visitors from around the globe.

b. YOUR SHOW OBJECTIVES

Wherever you may be exhibiting, being able to write orders at a show is a bonus. Unfortunately, many cultures prohibit this, at least initially. In Latin America, for example, you'll find that potential buyers want to build a friendship before doing business with you. This can be frustrating until you condition yourself to accept and work with the local culture.

In Latin America you should look upon shows as an opportunity to "show and tell" — a time to introduce new products and gain exposure for your company. Even after the show is over you must persevere in your efforts to make business friends or you won't be regarded as a serious supplier.

In the Pacific Rim countries, shows offer an opportunity to see new technology, do market research, meet people, and find agents. Making appointments to see potential customers or agents is an acceptable practice and a way to establish your credibility — a necessary preliminary to doing business in these markets. Here they look for long-term business associates. You should be very sensitive to national traditions, culture, and values which can count as much as the quality of your product itself.

In Europe, writing orders at the show will happen, but only if your product is exceptional. Generally, European shows are places to be seen and to meet agents. However, they are not the place for short-term "fixes." Exhibitors should be prepared to spend up to five years marketing in a European country to achieve success — the key to success in this market being quality products and services.

c. AGENTS

In many countries, trying to go it alone is a formula for failure. To meet and service the local market you will have to secure the services of a local agent, distributor, or representative who is familiar with the market and its culture. An agent can be very helpful in overcoming the various restraints that national and local governments may place on imported goods.

Trade shows are an excellent place to meet these intermediaries and in some countries your relationship with them is as important as your eventual relationship with the customer. In Latin America you can invite agents to come to your booth and see your products. The same holds true for Asia Pacific and Europe, but don't sign up the first agent that shows an interest. The appointment of an agent becomes a legally binding agreement in many countries and most agents are looking for long-term relationships. Before you bind yourself to any agents, check their credentials very carefully and also the local laws covering such agreements.

Local authorities often have a high regard for these relationships and support them to the letter of the law. In Latin America you could be obligated to pay commissions to an agent for up to two years after your agreement is terminated. Contracts must be very specific and in some cases registered with the local authorities.

In Asia Pacific, your relationship with an agent is based on your ability to get along with each other — to enter into a harmonious agreement. Most agents are happy with a simple one- or two-page agreement which may sound vague to you: what they are looking for is the development of a sense of trust in your business dealings that will lead to a long-term relationship.

In Europe, where you could be dealing with prospects from as many as 30 or 40 countries, using agents, dealers, and representatives is a good idea. They are interested in products and services that can be sold profitably and that are of excellent quality. Your legal arrangements will vary from country to country; be careful and do your homework well.

d. BUSINESS ETIQUETTE

Business etiquette is the area where inexperienced exhibitors make their major mistakes. You must learn all you can about the traditions and business culture of the country you plan to visit — before you leave home. You have a ready source of information in the embassies and consulates of the countries you plan to visit, as well as your own government trade commissioners who cover the areas of interest.

In Latin America, business and pleasure are mixed. There has to be a special chemistry between buyer and seller for business to succeed. Latin Americans value their family and family life and the personal component is very important in these relationships. When your contacts talk about their families and ask about yours, you know that they are trying to establish a rapport with you. After two or three meetings, they will probably invite you to their homes, but first impressions are what count and will affect up to 90% of the business you will eventually acquire. Punctuality is also extremely important.

Hong Kong and Singapore have adopted many North American values and methods, but their cultural background is still strong. Japanese behavior follows rigid rituals and you should have a "greeter" at your booth who is fluent in Japanese. Address people by their titles — don't use first names, ever. If you are talking to the president of a company, address him or her as "President...."

Be careful of the little things, such as the way you handle business cards. In North America we often take a prospect's business card and scribble information on the back of it. But to Oriental business people, business cards are extremely important and must not be handled casually. They will hand cards to you with their right hand and expect you to take it in both hands and read it carefully and respectfully. A casual, joking manner is offensive and will lead the prospect to think that you do not take your products or services seriously.

With their long tradition of exhibiting, shows in Europe are sophisticated and businesslike. First names are out — always use a formal address such as Mr. or Mrs. With visitors coming from as many as 30 or 40 countries to these shows, the challenge to behave culturally correctly is even greater. The rules for good boothmanship given in chapter 9 should be followed scrupulously. Smoking and eating in your booth can have a disastrous effect on your success.

Handshaking is an internationally recognized method of greeting people. Handshakes should be firm without pumping of arms. Always extend your hand to a male visitor, but when greeting female visitors, be sensitive to the local culture and only extend your hand if the practice is acceptable.

e. DRESS

The basic rule for dress is universal: always look formal and neat. You have to look serious if you wish to be taken seriously. In Latin America, even if the weather is hot, you should wear a business suit. Women should not wear short skirts.

In Asia Pacific, if you are invited into someone's home or a restaurant, you will be expected to take off your shoes. They will be left neatly together facing the door. Make sure that your socks are presentable and have no holes in them.

In Europe, looking like a professional helps make that important, good first impression. In some industries, such as fashion, more daring attire is acceptable, but for most, the key words are "elegant but sober."

f. FOLLOW-UP

As was recommended earlier, before you venture into a foreign market, you should do some research on understanding how business is conducted in that market. Since most business will not take place immediately, a knowledge of how and when you will most likely obtain that business will help you to prepare an appropriate follow-up plan.

In Latin America, your business relationship is an extension of your personal relationship and it follows naturally that any promises you may make will be taken seriously. In Asia Pacific and Europe, your punctuality will also be noticed.

Immediately upon your return home, you should write to those who visited your booth thanking them for their visit and enclosing whatever you promised as a follow-up. And your promises had better be kept by the date you said they would. Most customers are looking for long-term relationships and it's these first few crucial steps that help to cement your relationship.

In some cases, your follow-up to a European buyer can be conducted on the phone or through the mail. It is recommended that you plan to stay after the show is over to conduct business, or plan a return visit.

g. USING BROCHURES

Your brochures are an extension of your company. They should be prepared and priced in accordance with local customs. The language should be the official language of the host country, as well as English.

In Latin America, business prospects will take your brochures seriously. To avoid embarrassing errors, have your brochures translated and edited in the host country. This will ensure that there are no mistakes in the technical terms used or the language. Remember that while Spanish is the language of most Latin American countries, the language of Brazil is Portuguese.

If you are exhibiting for the first time, you can take English brochures with a one-page translation that describes your product or service. After you have appointed an agent, you can print a new brochure in the language required and carrying your agent's name.

Don't make the mistake of one exhibitor who printed a toll-free number on his brochure in the mistaken belief that it would give easy access to their company for Latin American buyers. The potential customers were insulted — first because they didn't know what a 1-800 number was, and when they did find out, they found that the number was not accessible from their country.

In Asia Pacific, your brochures must answer the technical questions buyers may want to ask. Your brochures will receive careful and close scrutiny. In many cases the written word will be taken more seriously than the spoken word.

European buyers look for quality and service information in your brochures in addition to the technical description of your product. You may hand out brochures at your booth or mail them later. Either approach is acceptable. Because of the wide area from which European shows draw their audiences, it is probably better to mail brochures to prospects after the show.

h. DEMONSTRATIONS

People of all nationalities seem to have the same desire to see, feel, and experience your products in action. The guidelines on demonstrating given in chapter 5 apply internationally, but with the warning that any element of fun should be tempered in keeping with the more formal nature of shows in other countries. Buyers are more impressed with a serious presentation and the use of videos is widely accepted. (Make sure that your video is in the right format for the country in which you plan to present it.)

In Latin America, it is acceptable to have an attractive hostess who acts as translator, greeter, and demonstrator. In Asia Pacific, demonstrations are more commonly performed by women than by men. In Europe, a well-thought-out, professional demonstration will help attract visitors to your booth. If you hire someone locally, allow time to train him or her properly so that he or she can intelligently answer questions about your products or services.

i. PERSONAL SPACE

The need for physical space varies from person to person and from culture to culture. If you get too close, some people will feel uncomfortable. This hinders rapport-building efforts. Personal space is culturally derived and should be carefully researched and strictly adhered to. In Latin America, for example, there is comfort with closeness. Two men will embrace as a sign of friendship once rapport has been established (but not at the first meeting). But for all visitors, handshaking is mandatory.

In Asia Pacific, men and women bow as they greet each other. Men and women bow differently and you must respect the space they need to carry out this custom. This is a ritual and personal space is closely guarded.

In Europe, where people are more formal, take your cues from your visitors. It is customary for a younger person to be introduced to an older person. Once again, shaking hands is mandatory while personal space will be mapped out by the visitor.

j. GIFT GIVING

Gift giving is a sensitive area and must be handled with care and a knowledge of local customs and laws. In some cases, no gifts are allowed; in others, a simple but tasteful premium may suffice; in some formal situations, a specially wrapped gift may be appropriate.

In Latin America, there are no gift giving expectations. However, an invitation to lunch or dinner is appropriate. This becomes an opportunity to socialize with the conversation drifting from business to pleasure. Be very careful about trying to leverage your friendship and don't ask for the order after dinner.

In Asia Pacific, it is good to take along a gift for an agent or a new customer. Take something from your company; it doesn't have to be expensive, but should not be tacky. Gifts should be well wrapped and handled with care. Be careful of giving gifts in China where many buyers are government officials who are not allowed to accept gifts.

In Europe, there are no general rules for gift giving. A premium might suffice, or you might give your major prospects something that will remind them of you (e.g., a coffee-table book describing your country or city). Such gifts should be handled selectively, preferably as part of your post-show follow-up.

k. QUALIFYING AT YOUR BOOTH

No matter where you exhibit, you will still need to do some qualifying of your visitors. It is still necessary to maximize the efficiency of your time at the show and to avoid wasting the time of your visitors, as well as your own time. In Latin America, you cannot ask the question, "Are you the decision maker?" You will have to be more discreet and ask questions like, "What is the structure of your company?" or "Does your president do the purchasing?" or "How is the purchasing process done in your company?"

In Asia Pacific, you cannot qualify quickly and the decision-making process is hard to follow. For example, in Japanese organizations decisions are made from the bottom up. While the president of a company may not make decisions, the middle management people will and should be targeted. At the same time, don't offend the older persons in the company by ignoring them. They will at least be involved in the decision.

In Europe, you should show prospects that you are interested in their company and qualify with discretion.

I. VERBAL AND NON-VERBAL SIGNALS

Unless you understand some of the verbal and non-verbal signals that prospects send to you, mistakes are inevitable. Understanding starts with an introduction to the use of language and gestures. In Latin America eye contact is the first thing they will notice, but simple things like pointing your finger and saying, "Please come here so that I can show you something," will turn off your prospect.

In Asia Pacific, the areas that require your understanding are names, food, dress, and talk. "Yes" can mean "no." There is no word for "no." They will say "Hai," which means "I understand you," or, "I hear

160

you." Because this is a highly ritualized society, respect for others is paramount, especially for the elderly.

Eye contact is important in Europe as is personal space. Don't crowd your visitors and avoid touching them.

m. FACILITIES

The biggest and best exhibition halls are found outside North America. Major shows can attract as many as two million visitors and receive world-wide coverage. In Latin America, the major shows are in the mining, plastics, communications, and food processing industries. Exhibitions are held in Brazil, Mexico, Panama, and Chile, to name a few.

China uses trade fairs as a major way of doing business. Their major centers are in Beijing, Guangzhou, Tianjin, Shanghai, and Shenzhen. In Beijing the major exhibition place is the CCPIT International Exhibition Centre which was opened in 1986. It has one-and-a-half million square feet of exhibition space.

Large shows in Hong Kong are held in the Hong Kong Convention Centre. In Japan it is the Nippon Convention Centre. In Singapore there are the World Trade Centre and the Chango International Exhibition. Other countries with large facilities in this region are Indonesia, Malaysia, Philippines, Taiwan, and Thailand.

Exhibition halls can be found in most major centers of Europe. For example, in Paris there is the Porte de Versailles; in Germany there are major fairs in Dusseldorf, Frankfurt, Hanover, Cologne, and other centers. Italy has its Milan Fairgrounds, while in England there is White City in London and the Convention Centre in Birmingham. Some of these facilities can cater to as many as 2,000 exhibitors.

When planning your show, it is important to check out the facilities very carefully to avoid last-minute problems. Check the details of floor loads, ceiling heights, lighting, air, water, and electrical loads. Material handling and audiovisual facilities should also be checked.

n. CONCLUSION

Your local consulate or embassy will have staff who can advise you on the appropriate behavior for the country you plan to exhibit in. Your library can also be a useful source of information and there are numerous books available in stores to help you understand the different cultures.

It is worth the effort to understand the people you intend to visit and do business with. Learn some of their language and customs; they will be pleased and it will help build the rapport necessary for a successful business relationship. The bonus for you is increased business opportunities and the excitement of learning about the many people who populate our planet.

PART II
AT THE SHOW

8

WORKING THE SHOW

a. SHOWS ARE NOT SALES CALLS

All the work and money you spent to date on selecting the right show, creating a winning booth, and developing a promotional plan will be wasted if the people working the booth do not know what to do.

Whether your objective is in the area of sales or in the area of communication, nothing happens until visitors are persuaded to make it happen. It is this process of persuasion that defines the interaction between booth people and show visitors. Understanding this role is a good beginning point. Salespeople know about persuasion, but some exhibitors feel their role at the booth is to disseminate information only and not to sell. This is far from the truth.

Selling a product, service, or new idea requires the same skill — persuasion. Prospects are unlikely to take any action if persuaders don't take care of their needs and establish a feeling of trust. Selling a product or service to new prospects, convincing visitors to take advantage of a new program, or convincing our kids to do their homework all require the same skills. In fact, we are all selling all the time. However, selling at a show is different from selling anywhere else.

At a show, selling isn't selling, it's boothing. Someone once said, "If people do what they always did, they get what they always got." When referring to successful salespeople placed in a trade show environment, this statement loses its validity. Often good salespeople do not make good boothers. Why? The rules change but the salesperson does not.

Unless salespeople understand this and adjust to the unique pressures of show selling, their chances of success are limited. Successful boothers are not developed overnight. It takes time, commitment, investment, and encouragement. So, let's begin.

Most salespeople are comfortable in normal business situations, in their clients' offices, in their own office, or on the retail floor. In these environments, they have time to develop a relationship with the prospects, they can comfortably determine their needs, and they can make a detailed presentation and close the sale. At a show, there simply is not enough time to accomplish this. This is the major difference between boothing and selling — your ability to adjust to time.

Let's examine this further. Here is an example. Think back to a time when you had a first meeting with a new prospect in your normal (non-show) environment. Your conversation probably revolved around the prospect's needs, your products or services, and included lots of social chitchat. No conversation is complete without talking about the weather, sports, current events, politics, movies, holidays, or the traffic. When we sit back and think about the time spent on nonbusiness-related issues, it might seem like a waste. However, it is anything but.

You include the social chitchat because your ultimate goal goes beyond the initial sale. Your focus is on developing a long-term business relationship. The reason for spending the seemingly unimportant time on nonbusiness-related subjects is sound. It is the search for commonalities between you and the prospect. The more things in common, the stronger the bond and the greater the likelihood for business.

Essentially, your job is to connect with people, to begin or continue building fruitful relationships. Salespeople who concentrate on only one sale at a time spend much unneeded energy. For them, every day becomes a new challenge void of the advantage of repeat sales and referrals. However, developing a solid business relationship built on trust and comfort ensures an ongoing relationship, post-sale contact, and new business opportunities, referrals, and testimonials.

At a show, the prospects have the same needs. We all want long-term business relationships. You want the business. You want prospects to take advantage of whatever you are offering. For your prospects, there is a real sense of satisfaction dealing with people they trust, and it makes shopping easier for them. They will go back to the person who treated them well because it is easier than starting all over again.

When I travel, I use the same airline, stay at the same hotels, and eat at the same restaurants because, as a busy traveler, I expect a certain level of service. People recognize me and my needs, and I feel confident that I will be taken care of. Many of us develop these kinds of shopping attitudes. The emotional aspect of business should never be overlooked. In many parts of the world, new business is solely dependent on positive feelings between people. It's all about building rapport.

b. RAPPORT BUILDING ON THE SHOW FLOOR

When it comes right down to it, people like to do business with people they like. Your first job on the show floor is to establish rapport and give prospective customers the impression that you are a person with whom they would like to do business.

The skill needed is called rapport building. Webster's dictionary describes rapport as "a harmonious or sympathetic relation or connection." It is a connection between two people who have a common bond and can share their commonalities. Once rapport is established, the talk flows easily, the communication channels are open, ideas are shared, and there is a positive feeling that gives each partner license to take risks with one another. In a business setting these risks are those we take when we share information candidly.

The social chitchat is your way of finding these commonalities and a familiarity that breeds a positive feeling. When there is a positive relationship, both customers and salespeople are more accepting of one another. It does not mean that they become complacent. However, there is now more to their business dealings than haggling over price. This positive feeling is what long-term business relationships are all about. Therefore, rapport-building skills are crucial to your success.

However, at a show, things are different. You do not have the time for all the social chitchat. Boothers who spend too much time with each prospect reduce the potential a show can offer. What is needed to succeed is to adjust your selling skills to cope with the scarcity of time.

If you still do not think there is a need to adjust your techniques, try this experiment. Ask your show organizer how many show visitors are expected. Let's assume 30,000 visitors are expected to attend over three days. If there are 25 show hours in total, you can expect an average of 1,200 visitors per hour, or 20 visitors per minute, to pass your booth. Obviously, if you deal with each visitor in the same as a sales call, you will simply not have enough time to deal with every visitor. Traditional rapport-building techniques simply go out the window. Building rapport with 20 people per minute seems impossible.

c. THE PITCHING TRAP

Time can be easily squandered. One common mistake many boothers make is to spend their time giving too much information to too many people who are not qualified. We have all seen this. Prospects innocently approach a boother only to find they are on the receiving end of a detailed explanation about the company's product or service. Or, prospects may have had legitimate questions that the boother answered in painstaking detail. The disseminating of information to people who may not be interested is known as pitching.

Boothers bring a great deal of knowledge about their products, services, and programs to a show and are looking for people to pass this along to. However, they have no real way of knowing what information prospects want, how prospects will use it, or if prospects have any real level of interest. All they know is that before them stand warm bodies to talk to.

The downside of pitching is an acceleration of the effects of trade show burnout (TSB). TSB is a result of working long hours on your feet and talking to a lot of people in a hectic environment. All boothers suffer from TSB at one time or another. However, pitching accelerates the effects of TSB. As has been often said, "It is all a matter of working smarter rather than harder." TSB is discussed in more detail in chapter 9.

There is another downside to pitching. Prospects might perceive you as being unprofessional. Prospects who are inundated with product information they didn't ask for perceive that you are trying to hard-sell them. You look desperate for business and may become a good candidate for unnecessary quibbling over things such as price.

Let's assume your product or service is a good one and is available at a fair price. Remember though that your prospects will want to do business with people they like. When pitched unnecessarily, prospects become skeptical, and the result may be lost sales.

Try another experiment. Think about the last time you purchased something from someone with whom you like to do business. For this exercise it doesn't matter whether it was a business-related purchase or a personal one. What did you like the most about the salesperson?

When I ask this question in my seminars, participants list professionalism, good listening skills, not too pushy, thorough product knowledge, enthusiasm, and caring.

Attendees come to shows to find products, services, and answers. They also come to meet people to deal with after the show. Attendance figures are growing because attendees get an additional value from attending that is lacking in other marketing alternatives: experience. Attendees come to shows to experience products and services and to meet the people who sell and service them. Shows are a face-to-face marketing forum where the attendee can see, feel, taste, smell, and hear. Does the receiver on the telephone feel right? Does the car door sound right when closed? Does that new food product smell right? And does doing business with the boother feel right?

Attendees want to deal with individuals, not the organizations they represent, because companies, institutions, and governments can be big, cold, and impersonal. People chose to do business with people they like who represent products and services they feel good about. Understanding this tells you that the people who work the booth are crucial to the show's success.

d. YOUR JOB DEFINED!

Your job is now defined simply as "getting people to like you." Don't confuse this with your objective, which is to collect a specific number of qualified leads, write a certain number of orders, or find dealers and representatives. The way you realize these objectives is through people. If people don't like you and the way you do business, you will not be successful. It's as simple as that. How do you get people to like you? Simple. Build rapport. Be the kind of person with whom they want to do business.

171

9

THREE BARRIERS TO BUILDING RAPPORT

Most salespeople practice good rapport-building habits in normal situations. However, in the show setting these good habits often go out the window for three major reasons: time, fatigue, and attitude. A look at each of these reasons will help you develop some skills to accomplish your objectives.

a. TIME

We now know time is a barrier. Building rapport with the kind of volume a show provides seems impossible. The obvious conclusion is that you can't deal with everyone who passes by. You are going to need to be selective. The trick is determining who you should spend time with. Sounds simple enough but it is highly unlikely you will be able to spot these visitors without asking a few questions. Qualify every visitor and you will know who to spend your time with.

The task of qualifying will consume most of your time at the booth. Your time will be spend culling through the sea of visitors looking for those you can help. You should not take any kind of action unless you know how qualified the prospect is. That's what qualifying is all about — determining who you should spend time with and how to spend that time most productively.

For many, this is a departure from the norm. Your natural inclination is to share information about your products or services. If the attendee asks questions, the obvious response is to answer with as much detail as possible. There are three problems with this approach.

(a) Attendees don't always know how your products, services, and programs can solve their need.

(b) Attendees will be suffering from information overload and you will be adding to it.

(c) You don't know how or why attendees need this information.

In the first few minutes of any interaction, you should take the role of information getter rather than information giver. Gather information and you will be able to address the prospect properly. If the attendee asks a question, a short answer followed up with another probing question will suffice.

The information gathering process has four distinct parts:

(a) an effective approach,

(b) a quick qualification

(c) the presentation, and

(d) the disengagement.

Each part of the process has its own agenda, so it is important to master each. It is also important to find ways of asking questions that you will be comfortable with. Think of the examples in this book as guidelines to help you develop questions that will feel right for you. Throughout the book, take advantage of the spaces provided to develop questions that fit your personality and your specific situation.

b. FATIGUE

The second barrier to rapport building at a show is fatigue. All exhibitors, at some time or another, fall victim to fatigue. Long show hours spent standing on your feet talking to scores of prospects takes its toll. Part of the challenge you will face is coping with the fatigue as best you can. Remember, your non-verbal behavior, which is hard to mask, reveals your true feelings. Customers and prospects need to feel confident in your ability to act as a professional, and much of their impression comes from what you do rather than what you say. Controlled non-verbal behavior can make the difference between a successful show and a failure.

Fatigue is a double-edged sword. It is not only your fatigue that gets in the way, visitors' fatigue also is a disturbance. Visitors have had a tough day too; they have worked the show, attended workshops, and talked to lots of exhibitors. Chances are that they are getting to a point where their fatigue will become a hindrance to you.

1. Coping with your fatigue

Many exhibitors get to the point where their fatigue hinders their ability to make good business judgments. Shows are filled with exhibitors leaning on furniture, sitting on chairs, flaking out, and generally giving the visual message, "I'm tired and burnt out."

174

Common sense should prevail, but it doesn't. Experienced exhibitors know that working a show properly requires an above-average ability to cope with physical, mental, and emotional stress. Coping with stress over a period of two, three, or ten days cannot be accomplished without some adjustment. The solution is pacing.

Athletes know about pacing. Before a challenging situation, athletes go into training to get themselves into peak shape. While business people readily learn new marketing and sales skills, they rarely develop the skills to handle show stress. Most business people will not do the kind of preparatory work an athlete does.

You need to exercise common sense. Working on your feet for six to eight hours in uncomfortable shoes, speaking to everyone who passes by, and eating lots of junk food is bound to have a price. So, pace yourself.

A number of commonsense rules have been developed by successful exhibitors over many years. None of these rules are based on rocket science but for the unprepared exhibitor, not following the rules can be disastrous. Here are some guidelines for pacing yourself at a show.

- *Get plenty of rest.* Having a good booth schedule gives exhibitors time to recharge their emotional and physical batteries. Often shows have an exhibitors' lounge which is a great place for tired exhibitors to get a few minutes of well-deserved rest.

- *Eat properly.* Often the food available at shows is designed as a quick meal for visitors. When you spend three or four days wolfing down quick meals, your body rebels. Take some time during the day to have at least one or two nutritious meals. A good breakfast gets the day off to a proper start, and a well-balanced dinner that you can eat slowly is a great way to reward yourself for a hard day at the show.

- *Avoid excessive after-hours partying.* The temptation will be there, and there *are* some positive benefits to attending parties, hospitality suites, and industry banquets. But you can't go to them all. If you are at an evening event, try to avoid the morning shift at the booth. You need to have enough energy to do the show properly, and you won't have it on a couple of hours sleep and a hangover.

- *Wear comfortable shoes and clothes.* You wouldn't climb a mountain in slippers, so why work a show in shoes that are not comfortable? Stand for eight to ten hours in new leather shoes and you are asking for sore feet and blisters. Wear comfortable shoes that are appropriate to your show and have already been broken in. Your feet will thank you. The same goes for clothes. Clothes that are restrictive will make you irritable and edgy.

- *Keep to a booth schedule.* Arrive for your shift on time, or preferably, a few minutes early. This is in fairness to your colleagues who have already put in a grueling shift and do not need the added pressure of worrying about booth relief. And when your shift is over, get out of the booth. Put your feet up and relax — your body deserves it.

- *Follow the rules of good business behavior and etiquette.* These rules cover mannerisms, behavior, appearance, and attitude.

2. Dealing with attendees' fatigue

By the time attendees get to your booth they will have been inundated with information gleaned from other exhibitors, as well as from workshops. They have been on their feet all day. Some are suffering from jet lag, others from exhaustion at the sheer magnitude of the show. Their fatigue might take the form of impatience, shortness of temper, or outright rudeness, leaving you wondering what brought them to the show in the first place. But, these visitors are not there to waste time: they have attended the show for a reason.

The best way to cope with attendees' fatigue is by respecting their time. Nothing drives visitors crazy as fast as inexperienced booth people who waste their time with things they are not interested in. Remember the dual purpose to information gathering?

3. Overcoming trade show burnout

Doing a show properly is stressful and the result can be trade show burnout. Trade show burnout (TSB) is simply your body telling you it has had enough and needs a break. Your feet and back might ache and your head might be pounding. TSB will have an effect on your ability to exercise common sense and your behavior will reflect this.

Often exhibitors suffering from TSB silently wish that all show visitors would simply vanish. If this sounds like an exaggeration, just walk a show and see some of the less-than-professional behavior some boothers express. TSB is lurking around every corner, so some preventative measures are in order.

The first thing you need to do is enjoy yourself. Have some fun and put some sparkle into the serious business of selling. The people you work with and the people you deal with will feel your enthusiasm and respond to it. It's a positive way of building rapport.

The second thing you need to do is be a good customer server. Don't let TSB make you lose sight of this important point. All your efforts to get customers and prospects into the booth are to no avail if you don't service them properly. Once visitors enter your booth, they should receive attention right away. Your attention to visitors will make the difference between so-so results and excellent results. Let's take a look at what constitutes good customer service at a show.

- *People waiting.* If you notice visitors waiting, you should at least acknowledge them with a nod of the head or a smile. Better still, say something like, "I'll be with you in a minute."

- *Refreshments.* If you provide some form of refreshments, be a gracious host and make sure they are offered to everyone who visits you.

- *Keep your promises.* Promises made to prospects are important, whether you make them at a show or elsewhere. Take care of them immediately after the show.

- *The golden rule: Do unto others as you would have them do unto you.* Make sure your service pleases your visitors in the same way you like to be treated. Remember that people really want to do business with people they like.

- *Develop good booth skills.* You can't act the same way with a show client as you do with other clients. Trade shows are not sales calls. Your job is to hone your skills to the challenge of show selling. Practice ahead of time so you can approach, qualify, disengage, and follow up properly. Do this and you will be a true show professional.

Overcoming the barrier of fatigue is nothing more than an exercise in common sense. But once at a show we tend to forget this. If you really want to excel at your next show, remember these simple guidelines.

c. ATTITUDE

Attitude is the third barrier to rapport building on the show floor. Not visitors' attitude but yours. We have all seen people working a booth who look tired, uninterested, bored, pre-occupied, or simply appear not to care. What is your impression of these people and the companies they represent? Negative, I imagine. The right attitude at a show sends a message to attendees that you are the kind of person they will want to do business with. Slouching, doing back stretches, or eating lunch does not reflect this message. The rapport-building process starts long before you engage in a conversation. It begins the second visitors walk by and see you — it's their first impression.

1. The do's and don'ts of exhibiting

Whether you have an opportunity to engage in conversation or not, the rapport-building process is taking place. Many attendees will look at you and your colleagues, and if your booth behavior is less than what they expect, they will simply walk on by. A look at the do's and don'ts of exhibiting will help you get your fair share of the show traffic.

Most of these rules are no more than common sense. But in a show setting when you are experiencing fatigue, common sense is sometimes hard to find. Building rapport is something you strive for in normal situations, but at a show where time is working against you, good rapport-building skills can go out the window.

If you have visited a show lately, you will probably remember exhibitors you didn't approach because they were too absorbed in conversations with each other, or eating their lunch, or doing paperwork, or obviously nursing a hangover, or because their appearance simply wasn't professional.

These exhibitors have an attitude problem. They have forgotten why they are exhibiting in the first place — to do business. Exhibiting is a change from your normal routine, but that doesn't mean it's a day off, or an excuse to party all night long. Make no mistake, working an exhibit is hard work and requires the same focus and professional behavior you would display in your normal work environment.

(a) Do's

- *Know your products and services.* Take time before the show to thoroughly familiarize yourself with all the products or services you are selling.

- *Be honest.* If you don't know the answer to a question, don't fake it. Don't try to con your prospects. Instead promise to get answers and follow up right after the show.

- *Know the booth.* Spend time learning all you can about your booth before the show starts. Know where everything is kept, how displays work, and how to arrange for show services if needed.

- *Know the show.* Be able to help out prospects with directions to washrooms, telephones, meeting rooms, exits, and eating areas.

- *Be well groomed.* Choose your attire carefully to suit your audience. Your appearance should be appropriate to the show, audience, and location, and it should reflect your professionalism.

- *Be confident.* Your confidence comes from being prepared.

- *Keep your booth neat and attractive.* With crowds of people flowing through your booth, your booth needs constant attention. It should always look as neat and tidy as it did when the show opened.

- *Treat all visitors equally.* Everyone deserves your respect. Don't fall into the trap of snap judgments about people. If you treat everyone with

181

the same respect and attention you will be pleasantly surprised at your results.

(b) Don'ts

- *Don't smoke.* A lot of people find tobacco smoke annoying or repulsive. If you can't wait four hours for a cigarette, arrange a two-hour shift. After your break, be aware of the smell left on your breath and your clothes.

- *Don't sit.* Chairs in your booth are for visitors, not for you. Don't sit down during your shift; be ready to greet visitors — on your feet.

- *Don't drink.* This means any kind of beverage. Alcohol is definitely a no-no and spilled coffee can damage your display.

- *Don't talk with colleagues.* People are reluctant to interrupt others. If you must have a conversation with a colleague, don't be so engrossed that you ignore waiting prospects.

- *Don't leave your booth.* Prospects who have taken the time to visit your booth deserve to have someone there to greet them when they arrive.

- *Don't go into someone else's booth unless invited.* This may be one of the written or unwritten rules of a show. Either way, it's common courtesy.

- *Don't knock the competition.* Never say negative things about your competition. People want facts, not your opinions.

Non-verbal messages have a powerful impact on your visitors. Research has shown that visitors find that the actual words spoken account only for 7% of a person's impression of you. The rest comes from your paraverbal — your tone of voice, inflections, volume, and pace, which accounts for 38% of the impression — and the non-verbal — your posture, gestures, and eye contact, which account for 55%. Because 93% of visitors' impressions happens on a non-verbal level, you need to be aware of your non-verbal messages.

The people we want to do business with are people we like. People we trust. People with whom we feel some rapport. People like to do business with people who are like themselves. This point cannot be made too many times.

The ability to develop rapport is a crucial skill in any place or business. At a show you must move quickly to create a friendly, relaxed atmosphere that is conducive to conversation. To understand your prospects' needs and wants, you have to "get into their heads" quickly.

The next chapter, Assessing Your Potential Customers, discusses in detail three categories of visitors — the visual, the auditory, and the kinesthetic. It will also discuss how you can develop your skill in identifying which category your prospects fall into, and how to use this knowledge to your advantage.

10

ASSESSING YOUR POTENTIAL CUSTOMERS

The grey cells inside your prospects' heads are no more mysterious than a basic computer. They respond to commands. To function, they are programmed by genetics, life experiences, and personal needs. As children, programming came from the environment, from things such as temperature, food, wetness, and so on. These are all things the infant had very little control over.

As adults, we have more control over what goes into our computer, but sometimes, older, poorly installed programs block access to new information. However, we have the power to delete and re-program our brain by removing the negative messages and replacing them with positive messages. Through our powers of persuasion we can edit, reformat, and totally change a visitor's point of view.

Every human being responds to clues that are based on senses: visual, auditory, olfactory (scent), gustatory (taste), and kinesthetic (feeling or touch). If you are primarily a visual person you will learn more quickly if you can see or picture something. Therefore, your brain will respond to visual commands. People who are primarily auditory may "hear" what you are saying but not "see" the point.

As salespeople we can move the persuasion process along faster by understanding which of the prospects' senses are being accessed at the moment they are being exposed to new information. It's just like a computer. Feed it information it can compute and you have the machine working positively. Feed it junk and there is no telling what kind of garbage it will spew out. By understanding your prospects' computers you have a powerful tool to use in the show setting.

How do you quickly learn what your prospects' thought processes are? Two California researchers, Richard Bandler, a linguist, and John Grindler, a mathematician, studied the relationship between the language people use and their thought processes. They called their research neuro-linguistic programming (NLP). Some NLP skills are perfectly suited to the show environment. Master some of these skills and your results will come quickly and easily.

These two researchers found that some people reacted more strongly to visual stimuli: a picture, photograph, or illustration. Others reacted more strongly to auditory stimulation: a graphic description or detailed explanation of the subject. People in a third group relied on their feelings about a subject or situation. If they felt good or had a warm feeling about something, their reaction would be positive. If they felt bad or had cold feelings about the subject, their reaction would be negative.

Most people respond in varying degrees to each of these stimuli, with one sense usually being dominant. Understanding which is dominant will help you relate better to your prospects. To find out which sense is dominant for you, try the following simple experiment.*

Read the next line, close your eyes, and note your reaction.

Think about your first car

What happened? Did you see the car's gleaming chrome, the glowing colors, and the glistening spokes?

Did you hear the roar of the muffler, or the scream of burning rubber, or the radio belting out the latest rock number?

Or did you again experience the great feeling of owning your own set of wheels, of being independent, of appearing "cool" to your friends?

The chances are that you reacted in varying degrees to each of these stimuli but one was probably much stronger than the other. If you are not sure, try the experiment again:

Think about your last business meeting

or

Think about your last holiday

What happened? Did you get a glimpse of the white sand beaches, palm trees swaying in the breeze, and the rows of sleek white yachts docked in a nearby harbor? Did you hear the band playing or the chatter of friends in conversation? Perhaps you felt the warmth of the afternoon sun or the cool rush of water on your skin as you jumped into the ocean. One of these statements will

---

* *reproduced with permission from the NLP Institute of Canada*

likely be more accurate for you than the others. Whichever statement is accurate for you reflects your primary mode of information accessing.

By understanding how your prospects process information you can present information in a way that is compatible to their modes of access. If your information is easy to understand, you will eliminate the mental struggle to comprehend. Present it without regard to their accessing strategies and the chances of misunderstanding are great.

Before looking at ways to discover a person's primary mode of access, make sure that you understand how each of these modes operates.

(a) *Visual.* Visuals are those people who understand what they see, rather than what they hear or feel. They take words and translate them into meaningful pictures. Without these pictures, words mean little to them. Even Einstein was visual and, according to reports, developed his theory of relativity by seeing himself riding invisible waves through the universe.

If you inhibit visual people from visualizing, you will not have rapport and most likely will not make the sale.

(b) *Auditory.* Auditories are influenced by sounds They respond to things such as voice inflections, rhythm, tone, pitch, and volume. These people interpret what they hear as positive or negative.

(c) *Kinesthetic.* People in this group rely primarily on their feelings to help them decide a course of action. Before kinesthetics buy, they must feel good about their decisions. Many home owners know this; when buying a new home it is often the house that "felt right" that ended up the winner.

If you can find our how your visitors access information it will help you develop rapport and build trust faster. People do not buy words. They buy trust. Visuals trust by seeing pictures, auditories by hearing the right sounds, and kinesthetics by trusting their feelings.

Bandler and Grindler found many clues to the way people access information. One of the most revealing involved changes in the subjects physiology. Changes in head movements, breathing, tonality, muscle tone, hand and arm positions, skin color, and the use of predicates all provide clues. Recognizing these can provide a powerful tool in your sales arsenal. So, let's look at each in turn.

a. HOW TO RECOGNIZE A VISUAL

Visuals understand what they can see. External stimuli are interpreted as pictures in their minds that work like a silent movie — one frame at a time. As you talk to them, they see a series of pictures rolling past their mind's eye. Here's how you spot them. (**Note:** The following discussion on eye movement applies to right-handed people. Left-handed people will react exactly opposite.)

(a) Eye movements:

Up and to the left: This eye movement tells you that they are seeing something in their past — they are reconstructing something that was triggered

188

by your conversation. Now is a great time for you to say, "Tell me something about your office or factory," because they are remembering.

Up and to the right: This movement tells you that they are constructing or creating a picture of the future. With this clue you might ask, "How do you see this fitting into your plans?"

(b) Head movements: For the visual, head movements tend to mirror their eye movements.

(c) Breathing changes: Visuals are generally shallow breathers and tend to stop breathing when they are accessing information. Since clothes tend to mask body movements, it is often difficult to recognize this clue in a visual. The easiest way is to watch their shoulders against a solid background.

(d) Tonality changes: Visuals can be spotted by their high-pitched or nasal tones.

(e) Tempo changes: Watch for quick bursts of words and a fast pace.

(f) Muscle tone changes: If you notice tension in the shoulders or abdomen, this is a clue that you are talking to a visual person.

(g) Hand and arm positions: Fingers are usually extended rather than clenched in a fist; arms are usually extended.

(h) Skin color changes: Some skin color changes can be subtle but observable to the alert salesperson.

Visuals lose blood from their faces when accessing information, resulting in a slight paling.

(i) Predicates: These are the verbal clues to a person's access mode. Visuals use words like see, aim, bright, clear, dark, dull, foggy, hazy, hide, image, light, look, observe, oversight, pattern, picture, view, and vision. These are visual words that describe the pictures in the prospect's mind.

b. HOW TO RECOGNIZE AN AUDITORY

Auditories interpret ideas through sound. They develop trust in a person through the way in which things are said to them. Sometimes, the way it is said is more important than what is said!

Everything you do with your voice helps the auditory person form an opinion.

(a) Eye movements: Auditories generally move their eyes from side to side. Sometimes these movements can be subtle so your powers of observation must be keen.

Left side: This movement suggests they are hearing past information. Try a question like this: "What did your partner say about the change?" If the eyes go to the left, the person is actually hearing the conversation he or she had about the change.

Right side: Movement to the right suggests construction. Try this test: ask, "What do you suppose people will say about this purchase?" If the eyes go to the right, the person is constructing a conversation that will happen in the future.

190

Down and to the left: When this happens, the auditory is usually involved in an internal dialogue. If you notice this behavior, it's a good time to stop talking and let the internal conversation run its course.

(b) Head movements: The auditory's head remains relatively level during conversation but moves from side to side in harmony with the eye movement.

(c) Breathing changes: A typical pattern is even breathing in the whole chest and diaphragm with prolonged exhalation.

(d) Tonality changes: The clue here is a clear, resonating tone.

(e) Tempo changes: Auditories talk in an even, rhythmic tempo.

(f) Muscle tone changes: Look for minor body rhythms and even body tension.

(g) Hand and arm positions: You'll receive a lot of hand and arm signals from auditories. Look for hands and arms folded, head tilted onto arms (the telephone position), hands touching mouth or chin, or counting with their fingers.

(h) Skin color changes: None that is noticeable.

(i) Predicates: Listen for the following words: argue, debate, discuss, hear, listen, loud, notice, quiet, ring, say, silent, sound, talk, tell, and verbalize. These are the kinds of words that describe an auditory's mental world.

c. HOW TO RECOGNIZE A KINESTHETIC

Kinesthetics are emotional people. They make their decisions based on how they feel about the person who is trying to communicate with them. They respond to hunches, gut feelings, instincts, and attitudes. Here's how they signal their mode of access:

(a) Eye movements:

> *Down and to the right:* This indicates that the person is accessing information that is either tactile (relating to the touch), or visceral (gut). This is a good time to ask, "How do you feel about making this purchase?"

(b) Head movements: Follows same direction as the eyes.

(c) Breathing changes: Watch the stomach. Kinesthetics are generally deep breathers.

(d) Tonality changes: These people have low, deep-toned voices and except for the occasional outburst, their voices are more breathy.

(e) Tempo changes: Characterized by slow speech with long pauses.

(f) Muscle tone changes: Muscle movement indicates tactile accessing. An even relaxation of the muscles indicates some internal visceral accessing.

(g) Hand and arm positions: Look for upturned palms and bent arms.

192

(h) Skin color changes: Increased, fuller color is typical of a kinesthetic's face.

(i) Predicates: Look for feeling words such as cold, connect, feel, grasp, hard, hot, invite, link, rough, soft, solid, stiff, tender, touch, and warm.

Figure #10 should help you identify these different access modes. When the eyes move in the direction of the lines, they provide clues to the person's means of accessing information.

By identifying the type of person with whom you are communicating, you will be able to respond to them in a manner that they understand and appreciate. Selling is tough enough under normal circumstances. Why make it harder by saying to a kinesthetic, "Just picture

Figure #10
Understanding eye movement

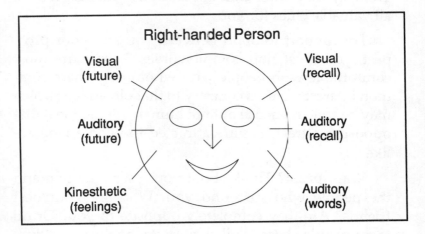

this!" The person can't and won't picture what you're trying to get across. They could, however, feel it.

Eye accessing is an easy skill to practice. Virtually everyone you meet, whether at a show, at home, or in the office, accesses information. Practice with everyone you meet until it becomes second nature to characterize a person according to his or her accessing mode, and to respond accordingly.

d. MIRRORING AND MATCHING

Once you know how your prospects access information, you are ready to go one step farther. You have already enhanced rapport by presenting information in a way that is comfortable to the way your prospects think. The next step is to reinforce that rapport with methods comfortable to the way your prospects act. Your prospects' personalities are expressed in their physiology. The way they walk and talk and carry themselves are all valuable clues for you.

For rapport to build between you and your prospect, you must find commonalities. People are most comfortable with people with whom they share common interests. This is contrary to that old adage (which may be true in science but not human interactions) that opposites attract. We are attracted to people who are like us.

Want proof? Think about your own situation and the people who surround you. Who are your best friends? Are they completely opposite to you? Or do these people share similar interests, hobbies, and lifestyles?

This is helpful information to have and something you intuitively know. In non-show situations you spend time finding things you have in common with your prospects. At a initial meeting with a prospect you discuss a variety of topics to see what you have in common. If you and I first met we would be total strangers. But during the course of our conversation you would probably find out that I am a baseball fan. If you are also a baseball fan we would very quickly become "baseball buddies." It becomes the foundation for us to further develop our relationship. As our relationship builds we would find other things we had in common. The more we share, the better we feel about each other, and the stronger is our rapport.

At a show you do not have the time to talk about nonbusiness-related subjects. There are too many people and too little time. The skill of mirroring and matching is perfectly suited to this situation and will help you find out quickly the things you have in common. Those things that you can deal with under the constraints of time are found in our physiology.

You have become aware of the subtle changes people express in their physiology. Now we are going to put that information to further use. By matching their paraverbal and non-verbal actions, you are sending a clear message that you have things in common. If prospects are very demonstrative, with lots of hand gestures, you will use lots of hand gestures. If they talk softly, so will you. This is not mimicking. You are not copying your prospects' actions exactly, rather, you are only matching observable behavior. A slight modification will do the trick.

While you are mirroring and matching, you never change your moods or lose who you really are. Mirroring and matching is something you do all the time. We all change our behavior each time we interact with someone. When you listen, look for clues, and consciously match, you are taking important rapport-building steps. Ignore the clues you see and you are building a wall between you and your prospects. Pick up on the clues and match them and watch rapport grow.

1. Matching paraverbal

Listen to your prospects. What do they do with their voices? Do they talk quickly or slowly? Is there a variation in their voices or are they monotone? Do they speak quietly or loudly? I have a colleague who is a public speaker. He has a loud booming voice that can be heard in all corners of a room. Seldom does he need a microphone. At the conclusion of a presentation he will invite members of the audience to meet with him if they have questions. After a presentation it is not uncommon to see dozens of people congregate around him with specific questions. However, I have seen people leave their spot in line when they realize that his voice had not changed. When I approached some of these people to ask why they left early, I noticed they were soft spoken. Regardless of the reason they gave, it soon became obvious that the thought of a conversation with someone loud was not appealing and perhaps even threatening.

Here is another example of mismatching. I had double parked my car to make a return of an item at a local store. Because I had double parked, I was in a hurry, and I tend to talk quickly, particularly when I am in a hurry. I entered the store and was immediately greeted by the clerk, who spoke very slowly, every word meticulously articulated. All I could do was watch my car through the store window to ensure it wasn't being ticketed. As soon as the clerk started talking I became agitated. He was efficient but our paraverbal actions were mismatched and rapport building was hindered.

To put your prospects at ease, listen for paraverbal clues and match their speech patterns. Talk slower or louder or whatever you have to do to let prospects know you are on the same track: You have something in common — you speak in a similar manner.

2. Matching vocabulary

Language is the way we let the world know what we are thinking. The words we choose represent the mode of accessing we are most comfortable with. Listening carefully will give us important clues to rapport building.

Language can be a major barrier to rapport if not handled correctly. Think back to your last vacation. If you were in a country where a language other than yours was spoken, you know how uncomfortable things could sometimes be. If someone didn't understand you, your immediate response was likely to repeat the question either louder or slower, neither being a good strategy, since the person didn't understand what you were saying in the first place. As you tried to communicate, you probably felt edgy with this person. There might have been an element of distrust, and certainly a feeling of unease.

Language is a key to the way we access information. It determines the way we express our views of the world. When people are goal-oriented, the words they use will be those that are goal-driven. "The task at hand is . . ." or "What's the bottom line here?" If people view the world in terms of the big picture, they might say, "Let's step back from this for a minute," or "Show me where this is going." Understanding how your prospects views their world can be determined from simple comments such as these.

A common mistake made by many is the use of jargon. Often colleagues will get together and discuss the days' problems, new developments, or product information. It is quite common and acceptable to use jargon specific to the industry in the conversation. However, once you leave this environment, other people don't understand what you are talking about.

On the other hand, you may have sophisticated clients who have had a lot of experience dealing with your company and products. To them, a conversation without the jargon would be an insult. They have grown comfortable with the language.

Sometimes you assume your customers' language: "All engineers will understand this . . ." Some will and some will not. The solution is to listen carefully to your prospects. Don't dazzle them with your fancy lingo. Instead, respond to their questions with intelligent answers in the same language they are speaking.

Language also involves word choice. You have already learned that your prospects' choice of words will give you clues of their mode of information accessing — visual, auditory, or kinesthetic. But words will reveal more. For example, words will indicate your prospects' level of commitment. Some people will use committed language — "I will," "I won't." Some will use less committed words, such as "I might" or "I shouldn't." Listening to the choice of words is insightful as you see a growing level of commitment from less to more positive words.

3. Matching non-verbal

"Non-verbal" refers to the way we use the rest of our body. Gestures, posture, facial expressions, breathing, physical distance, shaking hands, even the clothes you wear are all considered non-verbal language.

Watching and studying body language is interesting and an important part of your study of human nature. We all have a unique way of expressing things. In the past, much emphasis was placed on what our body language meant in concrete terms: crossed arms meant you were creating a barrier and were holding back something; rocking back and forth meant you were impatient and bored; avoiding eye contact meant you were not interested in what someone was saying.

Whether these and the many other generalizations you might hear are true or not is irrelevant. Your job is not to understand what your prospects' body language means, it is to make your prospects comfortable enough to want to do business with you. Mirroring and matching body language is reacting to what you see, rather than what you think it means.

Here are six samples body language to be aware of.

199

(a) Gestures: Some people are quite demonstrative. Others don't seem to know what to do with their arms and leave them at their sides.

(b) Posture: Some prospects have stiff posture and some are more relaxed.

(c) Pacing: Some prospects never seem to be able to stand still while others are cemented into one place.

(d) Clothes: Your dress tells people you are a professional and ready to do business.

(e) Physical space: Some prospects seem to be "in your face." They are in your physical space, while others keep a certain distance.

(f) Culture: Many of the ways body language is expressed is found in the various cultures of the people you talk to. If you are sensitive to these cultures you can use these gestures to your advantage.

11
ENGAGING VISITORS

a. THE APPROACH

Most of us are comfortable handling people in normal selling situations — in a client's office, in your office, or on the retail floor. Exhibiting is a different situation. You will be standing at your exhibit with dozens, maybe hundreds or even thousands, of people walking by. You have two choices: hang back and let visitors come to you, or proactively approach them.

Some visitors will make the first move. However, as often as not, visitors will resist making contact. Many visitors scope out the whole show before they commit to a long look at an exhibit; some are shy, some don't know who to talk to, some are simply overloaded with information, and some do not see a connection between their needs and your products. Take the initiative and approach the visitors.

Remember why you are at the show and stay focused on your objective. You are in the booth to do business. Being proactive at an exhibit will give you maximum advantage. You will not waste valuable opportunities hanging back and waiting for prospects to approach.

b. OVERCOMING TIMIDITY

Approaching is not as easy as it sounds. You need to overcome timidity, develop an effective opener, avoid closed questions, and focus on business. Your challenge is to do this while not appearing too pushy — the number one objection visitors have about show salespeople.

Many booth people do not feel comfortable being proactive. This is understandable. It may be an unfamiliar way of doing business. Further, there is the fear of being rebuffed, appearing pushy, or not knowing how to approach visitors gracefully. Reaching out to visitors is a compliment, an attempt to engage them in a conversation that nine times out of ten they will appreciate. However, it is one thing to approach visitors and quite another to do it comfortably and effectively.

c. EFFECTIVE OPENERS

Openers such as "Enjoying the show?" or "Pleasant day, isn't it?" or "Wasn't traffic a bear this morning?" are time-worn and ineffective and do not lead anywhere. Visitors can answer with one word and keep on walking. Worse yet, they can answer at great length and waste your time with irrelevant chitchat.

A good opener engages visitors in meaningful conversations about business and is a graceful beginning to the heart of your job: qualifying.

Effective openers waste no time. They get directly into the job of qualifying visitors. The best way to start is with a question about the visitor's needs. Your display focuses on the key benefit of your product or service. Questioning your visitor's need for this key benefit is the most effective way to launch your conversation. Here are a couple of examples:

"How often do you run into problems transferring business information from program to program?"

"Tired of paying an arm and a leg for quality widgets?"

d. AVOID IRRELEVANT QUESTIONS

As mentioned above, asking questions when you really don't care about the answer is a waste of everybody's time. This point is worth repeating. Questions about the visitors health or the weather don't get you into a meaningful conversation. (Unless you sell health or weather-related products). Irrelevant questions are too easy to ask.

Questions relating to booth activities (e.g., "Want to enter our draw and maybe win a trip to Hawaii?" or "Our next seminar is just about to begin and everyone who attends wins a great prize,") accomplish nothing and you may appear boring and insincere.

e. AVOID CLOSED QUESTIONS

Effective openers invite visitors to pause and continue the conversation. Closed questions, questions visitors can answer with a simple yes or no, will not serve you as well as questions that require a lengthier answer. These are open questions, questions usually beginning with words such as how, what, when, where, and why.

However, closed questions are not completely out of the question. But you do need to know where you are going by having a follow-up question that eliminates the possibility of being left in the lurch.

f. HAVE A FOLLOW-UP QUESTION

An exhibitor approached me once with the question, "Are you familiar with our company?" A good closed-ended question.

I said yes and the exhibitor answered, "That's great." Our conversation ended. What started out as a good opening question fell through because the exhibitor hadn't developed a follow-up response. If I had said no, the exhibitor should have answered, "Let me tell you about . . . ." If I had said yes, his next question should have been, "What have you heard about us?" In either case, the exhibitor would have engaged me in a meaningful conversation.

g. THREE APPROACHING SCENARIOS

A good approach does not need to be complicated. Be sure to use phrases you can say comfortably and honestly. There are three scenarios of approaching visitors on the show floor. A quick look at each will give you the necessary background to develop openers of your own.

The trick is to plan ahead and develop your openers before exhibiting. During the show you will have enough to think about without having to worry about opening lines. Prepare ahead of time so you become comfortable with the questions. Remember the Boy Scouts' motto: Be prepared!

1. Scenario #1: When visitors appear interested

When visitors approach your booth and appear interested in a product or your graphics — or anything in your booth — your job has begun. However, you cannot assume there is real interest. They might have stopped to rest, or been attracted by something irrelevant to your business, or want instructions from you about show amenities.

Waiting for visitors to make the first move is a waste of time. Instead, approach them with a business-related opener. A good opener focuses on what attracted them in the first place ("What cash management do you use now?"). Or, if you are not sure where their interest lies, ask, "What caught your eye?" or "What attracted you to my booth?" Don't forget to introduce yourself first!

Take a moment and create one or two openers that you might use in this situation.

_____

_____

_____

_____

2. Scenario #2: When you are conducting a demonstration

The second scenario can be divided into two sub-scenarios: (a) you are working the booth when someone else is conducting the actual presentation and (b) you are conducting the presentation yourself. Let's take a look at both situations.

(a) You are working the booth when someone else is conducting the demonstration

A demonstration will attract lots of people. As the demonstration is ending, look into the crowd and choose one person to approach. Although you have a number of people observing the demonstration, you need to pick the most likely prospect. The prospect you choose is the one who expresses more interest than others in the demonstration.

You can spot an above-average level of interest in many ways. Sometimes you will pick up positive comments and questions. Also look for nonverbal clues, such as a visitor nodding his or her head in agreement or leaning in closer or smiling. Trust your experience; it is good indicator when looking for positive interest.

Once you have identified your prospect, use signals you have a pre-arranged with the demonstrator and other booth staff which indicate, "This is my prospect." For example, you might move beside the prospect. Other boothers will see your positioning and keep away. Having signals eliminates the problem of too many boothers chasing the same prospects.

Once the demonstration is over, approach the prospect and ask, "What part of the demonstration was most applicable to your needs?" or "How does this product fit into your work needs?" or "What was the best part of that demonstration for you?"

Take time now to create opening lines you can use in this situation.

_____

_____

_____

_____

(b) If you are the demonstrator

When you are conducting the demonstration, look for the person who is expressing an above-average interest. Once you have spotted this person, don't stop the demonstration to approach the prospect and ignore the rest of the audience. Complete what you have begun. Remember, just because one person is demonstrating interest at a greater level than the others doesn't mean there are not other interested people watching the demonstration. You really do not know the level of interest in the crowd. You should complete the demonstration while giving your prospect a reason to stay.

Ensuring the prospect stays is a matter of understanding why he or she has attended the show in the first place. Earlier in this book you learned that a show is a face-to-face marketing forum. Visitors attend to meet representatives and to experience their products and services with all their senses (sight, sound, touch, taste, and smell). The best way to encourage the prospect to stay after the demonstration is to appeal to one or more of these senses. Let the prospect help you with the demonstration, taste the food product, turn on the machine, feel the sample, or touch the keyboard. An effective demonstration always includes audience participation, which enhances the quality of the demonstration and keeps the interested prospect around asking questions afterward.

Your approach line after the demonstration is similar to that used in the first scenario. For example, you might say, "How do you see this working in your factory?" or "What response would you expect from your staff if you introduced this process in your office?"

Take time now to create opening lines you can use in this situation.

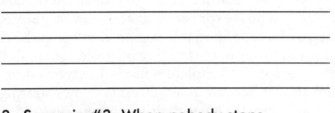

3. Scenario #3: When nobody stops at the booth

Your most challenging approach is needed when the booth is quiet and visitors do not come voluntarily. A quiet booth breeds bad habits such as slacking off, reading in your booth, making phone calls, or taking a coffee break. If you stay focused on your objectives, you are reminded that although the show is slow, your job still goes on.

If visitors are not coming into the booth, move to where they are: the aisle. But don't stand in the aisle; rather, stand at the edge of your booth or walk comfortably around its perimeter. Make sure you don't look bored. Don't get caught pacing uncomfortably. Relax, look approachable, and remember, a smile always helps.

The tool to work with is eye contact. Watch visitors pass by your booth and try to catch their eyes. Most visitors will ignore you. But don't let this discourage you, and don't take it personally. They might be distracted by other show activities, be talking to colleagues, be afraid of being trapped by unwanted salespeople, or simply be overloaded with information.

Research shows that the number of visitors who will walk by a booth and not return the exhibitor's eye contact can be as high as 95%. But once someone does make contact, be prepared with a simple opening question such as, "What are you looking for at the show?" or "I see you are in the printing business; how do you handle down time?" or "Have you found what you're looking for at the show?"

Take time now to create opening lines you can use in this situation.

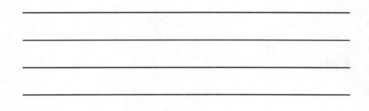

h. *PRACTICE, PRACTICE, PRACTICE*

For some, approaching visitors may be easy, for others it can be uncomfortable. For many, approaching strangers is a new skill requiring time, patience, and practice. There is also the fear of rejection. Your first try may not produce instant success. This does not mean you did something wrong. Rather, it is an indication that you need more time to master your technique.

Start with a simple approach and practice it. Be patient. Rome was not built in a day! Each time you try, you are one step closer to success. And the more times you are successful, the greater your comfort level. There is only one way to learn any new skill perfectly and that is to practice.

Once you have broken the ice with your prospect, the next step in the information-gathering cycle is to create a series of questions that let you decide how you will spend your time with the prospect.

12

QUALIFYING VISITORS IN FOUR MINUTES OR LESS

a. *SPEND AN APPROPRIATE AMOUNT OF TIME WITH EACH VISITOR*

The great thing about exhibiting is the sheer volume of people you can meet. It's your job to take advantage of these numbers. You can do this only by spending an appropriate amount of time with each visitor you approach.

"Appropriate" is something you will have to define. It will depend on your objective, the volume of traffic, and the time available. But, whatever you decide, demonstrating your product or service to visitors who have no use for it is bad time management. It steals time you could be devoting to visitors who might be prospective customers, and it steals time from your visitors who might be better off with another exhibitor.

Once you have made contact with visitors, the next job is to qualify them. Uncover certain key pieces of information which will tell you how best to proceed, and to do this as quickly and efficiently as possible.

The reason you spend time qualifying is twofold. First, qualifying lets you know how to properly allocate your time with each particular visitor. You need to know whether to proceed with a presentation or immediately disengage. Second, it ensures visitors that you understand their needs. Research shows that nearly 40% of all visitors will leave a booth without making any sort of commitment because they felt the boother had not taken the time to understand their needs.

b. ACTION

Gathering information about visitors is a matter of taking ACTION. ACTION is an acronym that contains six pieces of information boothers need to qualify a prospect:

1. Authority

2. Capability

3. Time

4. Identity

5. Operational constraints

6. Need

ACTION is a guideline for qualifying. Deciding how you can use each piece of information is important. Be flexible with each step. In some situations you may need all six items of information, in others you may not.

The order of information as presented in the ACTION acronym is not necessarily the order in which you must ask the questions. Pick the order that best works for you. Use ACTION as a guideline to creating your own qualifying questions.

1. Authority

One piece of information that will help you decide how to proceed is an understanding of your prospect's level of authority. You need to ascertain whether the prospect is a decision maker or decision influencer and how decisions are made in that prospect's company. Knowing this allows you to determine how to spend your time.

If the prospect is a decision maker and you choose to continue with the presentation, your objective, what you want from the prospect, is a decision.

If the prospect is a decision influencer, your objective is to get him or her to influence the decision by taking the information back to the decision maker.

Your words will be different in each scenario and you will be wasting valuable time using the wrong words. If you ask a decision influencer to make a decision, you are projecting a message that clearly says you have not taken the time to listen.

Questions such as, "Do you make the decisions on these products?" or "How are decisions made in your organization?" or "Will anyone else be involved in the buying decision?" will reveal the person's level of authority.

At a consumer show you will also need this information. If, for example, you are approached by a couple, do not hesitate to find out who the decision maker is. Many boothers assume who the decision maker is and they often make mistakes. Level of authority has nothing to do with the product (men buy kitchens and women buy cars) and it has nothing to do with who is asking the question and who is listening. Simple questions such as, "Are you both involved with your family's financial planning?" or "Did you both get involved with last year's vacation plans?" should reveal the level of authority.

If the answer is, "We are both involved in the decision," fine! If the answer is "No, my wife looks after that," this is not a signal to ignore the husband. It *does* mean you will have to make sure the wife is involved in every step of the process.

Years ago I attended a car show with my wife. We were there to check out the new models. Here was a great chance for her to find a replacement for the eight-year-old car which was now costing her more than it was worth to maintain. Barbara is a career woman and my partner in business. As she wandered around the car show, a new model in one of the displays caught her eye. I had gone off somewhere else to check out another car that we clearly couldn't afford (but that's another story).

The car Barbara was interested in was marked "prototype." Barbara went to the information booth and approached a consultant in a white coat who was busy ignoring her. He abruptly looked at this lone female and asked, "What do you want?"

"I want some information on that car over there," Barbara replied.

"Talk to a salesman," he said, "I'm here from production."

"Look," Barbara said as her anger built, "I just need to know a few things about that car. It looks like everybody is busy. Can't you just answer a few simple questions?"

At this point, the man looked at her and asked, "Where is your husband?"

Needless to say, Barbara didn't buy that car. Not only that, she has repeated this story as many times to other people as have I. No telling how much damage that one comment caused. The bottom line is: don't assume the level of authority.

Warning: Once you know who the decision maker is, never ignore the decision influencer. That person is still a valuable part of the process.

Take time now to create questions you can use in this situation.

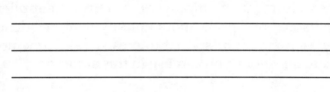

2. Capability

Does your prospect have the capability to buy and use your product? If you define capability as affordability, questions related to money are important. But there is often more to capability than money. Understanding how people might use your product or service will give you clues that will help you connect more firmly with the prospect. For example, if you are selling a financial product, understanding the prospect's level of sophistication is important. You certainly do not want to be caught talking down to a sophisticated prospect. On the other hand, you could inadvertently fill your presentation with ideas and jargon that are clearly beyond the grasp of the less-experienced prospect.

Start by asking questions dealing with budgets. For example, "Have you allocated a budget for this purchase?" or "What price range are you considering?" Remember you are still at the beginning of your interaction with this prospect, so asking detailed questions about finance is inappropriate. Chances are the prospect will not have the confidence in you to give you accurate information. All you should aim for at this point is an understanding of the prospect's approximate level of capability.

Questions revealing something about the prospect's history will let you know if you are in the right ballpark. Ask business prospects about size of company, years in business, number of employees, or current suppliers. Ask personal prospects about employment, residence, lifestyles, hobbies, or special interests. Take time now to create questions you can use in this situation.

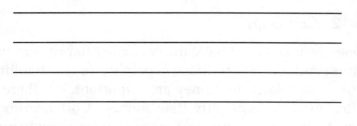

3. Time

Time is always a challenge. If you have done your job properly, you will leave the show with lots of good leads to follow-up. Your next task will be placing these leads in some order of priority.

Which lead is your number one priority? You might be tempted to choose the prospect with the potential for the largest financial return. Some salespeople will prioritize according to prospects they like and place the easiest to get along with on the top of their lists. Both these approaches have merit. But your real criteria should be based on time.

We know that people are most likely to make purchasing decisions quickly after a show; therefore your top priority should be those contacts who need you the soonest. It doesn't mean that you ignore or delay contact with the other leads, it just means that those with a time constraint should be handled quickly. Visitors leave a show with expectations and are ready to make a post-show buying decision. If you don't get back to them quickly, your competitors will. Ask questions such as, "When are you considering adding this new technology?" or "When is the next 'open to buy'?" or "How soon would you like to begin?"

Take time now to create questions you can use in this situation.

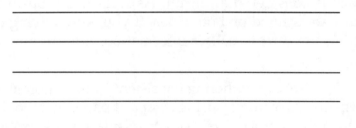

4. Identity

Knowing your prospect's name helps you build rapport. If your show registers its visitors and gives them a badge, the job is easy. If not, simply introducing yourself or exchanging business cards will give you the information you need.

But getting the name is not enough. You need to gather information and record it in an organized manner so you can follow up successfully. If you have future plans with the prospect, having additional information recorded will be an asset.

Your business relationship starts the moment you first meet. If you leave a prospect with a positive feeling when you call after the show and then proceed to ask all the same questions again, you are giving the prospect the wrong message. Everyone wants to be recognized. No one wants to be relegated to being a number. Your contacts deserve more. So you need to record everything they tell you.

Relying on business cards, scraps of paper, notebooks, or worst of all, your memory, places you at a disadvantage. The problem with business cards is twofold. First, in many cultures, business cards are an important document. For many it is a reflection of their personality. Flipping a card over and writing on the back is considered an insult. As well, many business card are printed on both sides. If you were relying on using the card to collect information you are now in trouble.

You are not gathering consistent information in an organized fashion by using scraps of paper, notebooks, and your memory. These can be misplaced or forgotten and create a follow-up headache. To remember all the information you are collecting, use lead cards. These are a simple pre-printed forms that provide you with a place to record all pertinent information for follow-up.

218

The forms should be no larger than 3" x 5" so they can fit comfortably into a jacket or blazer pocket. Pad the forms with a cardboard backing so you have a built-in surface on which to write.

Include space on your lead card for recording anecdotal information volunteered by the prospect as well as any promises you have made.

You should complete the lead card immediately, while you are talking to the prospect. Use a lead card with each prospect during the qualifying process once the conversation is underway, and jot down all the information you are uncovering. If you feel awkward writing information while you are talking to a prospect, remember that most serious people will understand your need to gather information. The simple solution to your discomfort is to ask the prospect's permission to keep notes. A question such as, "Do you mind if I jot down a few notes while we talk?" should be adequate.

If you wait to record the information until after the prospect has left the booth, you run the risk of forgetting or confusing the pieces of information you have collected. A lead card is your most valuable booth tool (next to your booth people, of course). Sample #3 shows a sample lead card you might model yours after.

Many shows use a lead retrieval system. This system is appropriate only for shows where visitor registration is required. The lead retrieval system can take the form of a bar code machine, card swipe, computer number, or a number of other methods. It is your way of accessing visitors' registration information and saves you time gathering simple statistics from the visitors themselves.

Sample #3
Lead form

Name of Show_____Date _____

Is Prospect a Buying Authority?_____

Does prospect have the Cash?_____

Will prospect buy within Time period?_____

Identity:

Name_____

Title_____

Company_____

City_____

Province/State_____Postal/Zip code_____

Telephone (___)_____Fax (___)_____

Operational constraints_____

Need_____

Appointment made_____

Service offered_____

Other comments_____

_____

_____

_____

_____

Read your show manual carefully to determine if a system is available. Check the details carefully. Determine the ease of accessing information, the timing of information, the quality of the information, and its completeness. If you then think the system will make your job more efficient, go ahead and use it.

At some shows, the lead retrieval system will replace your lead card completely. Sometimes you will need a modified card with fewer questions. Some exhibitors use a lead card regardless of the information provided on the system so they can record anecdotal information and any promises they make.

Take time now to create questions you can use in this situation.

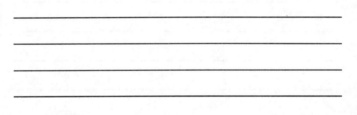

5. Obstacles

Boothers sometimes spend unnecessary time with the wrong prospect by ignoring the obstacle question. Obstacles are reasons that may prohibit the prospect from doing business with you. You have already learned the prospect's decision making ability, his or her capability to buy and use your product or service, and the timing of the purchase. You are recording all this information on the lead card. However, in every business there may be other criteria to explore, such as the size of the company, geographical proximity, long-term commitment with your competitor, previous experience with your product or company, territory restrictions, type of equipment, or political embargoes.

Every company has its own obstacles. Discover yours by asking simple questions that go directly to the point. For example, you might ask, "Where is your store located?" or "Who are you dealing with now?" or "Tell me a bit about your manufacturing process?"

Determining obstacles early in the interaction will save you valuable time both at the show and during your follow-up.

Take time now to create questions you can use in this situation.

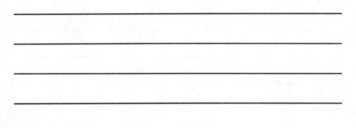

6. Need

At the beginning of the this section I mentioned that your questions can be in any order. Often, the Need question should be asked first rather than last, since determining if the prospect has a need for your product or service is crucial. When developing this question, take care. Need questions dealing with your need for being at the show are not the best use of your time. Questions such as, "Looking for a new word processor?" or "Want to save time with your manufacturing?," while addressing a need, often don't give you an opportunity to get the prospect opened up and talking.

You learned that nearly 40% of show visitors will not make a commitment because they perceive that the exhibitor has not taken the time to understand their needs. A question structured around prospects' needs rather than yours will solve this problem and be more productive. For example, questions such as "What brings you to the show?" or "Are you finding what you are looking for at the show?" go to the core of the visitors' need. It gets them talking and saves you valuable show time.

Take time now to create questions you can use in this situation.

_____

_____

_____

_____

c. CONCLUSION

Once you have the answer to the six questions, you will know how to proceed. By learning the prospects' level of authority, their capability to use your product or service, the time frame for decisions, and the prospects' identity, and you have identified any obstacles and understand the prospects' needs, you can go on to the next step. If the prospect is qualified, you will proceed with a quick presentation. If the prospect is not qualified, disengage. In either case, your time will be spent wisely.

13

MAKING THE PRESENTATION

The world's top chefs all know that the real secret of a successful dish is its presentation. The same holds true for marketers, salespeople, boothers, and consultants. However, often the preparation of a good booth presentation gets left to chance. The result is a presentation that is either too long or too short, too comprehensive or one that scarcely provides enough information for prospects to make a decision.

a. MAINTAIN YOUR FOCUS

Making presentations to people who have no use for your product or service is a waste of time. Making presentations without having properly qualified the prospect is also a waste of your time.

In your pre-show planning an objective was established for your exhibit (see chapter 1). This objective will keep you focused throughout every stage of your show participation, including the booth presentation. Although you need to be prepared to be flexible and discuss other products or benefits as dictated by your prospects' needs, a well-planned presentation helps you focus on your reason for exhibiting. Your presentation will lead to an immediate sale, an opportunity for a follow-up visit, or a request for more information.

b. TIME MANAGEMENT

As you create your booth presentation, remember that a show is big, noisy, and exciting. It's a place to capture visitors' interest, but is not usually the best place for a detailed discussion. For that, you will need the peace and quiet of a follow-up visit.

You should develop a presentation that works within your time constraints. If your objective is a lead to follow-up with later, a presentation attempting to tell prospects the whole story is overdoing it. You don't have to cover everything; merely whet the prospect's appetite. Your presentation should last about five to seven minutes. Doesn't sound like much time, but a well-structured presentation will cover a lot of ground in a short time.

If you put too much information into your presentation, it only confuses your prospects. Psychologists tell us the human brain can remember only seven pieces of information at one time. Tell prospects too much, and their chances of remembering it all are slim. Tell prospects the key elements and leave them wanting more in a follow-up visit, and you have done your job well.

If your objective is to make the sale, you need to put more time into the presentation and go into more detail. As a general rule, most products that are appropriate for immediate sale do not require excessive amounts of time to explain, so keep it as short and simple as possible.

c. PREPARING YOUR PRESENTATION

Remember the old newspaper formula, "Tell them what you are going to tell them, tell them, and then tell them what you have just told them"? This three-part formula follows the key functions of an effective presentation: the opening, the body, and the close. Each part has its own purpose and requires individual details.

d. THE OPENING: "TELL THEM WHAT YOU ARE GOING TO TELL THEM"

1. The bridge

The opening is a graceful bridge from qualifying into the actual presentation. It also focuses visitors on the needs your product or service can meet. Up to this point you have been gathering information. Now you are about to reverse the process and give some information. This bridge is important because you want to keep prospects moving along with you. The bridge could be as simple as, "Let me take a moment to show how our widget will help you accomplish the economies you are looking for."

2. Confirm the need

During the qualifying process you will have established your visitor's need. Now restate it.

Visiting a show is difficult and visitors often suffer from information overload. Don't add to the overload. The more you can organize information for them, the better. Help prospects by putting your information into a neat mental package. You might say, "I would also like to show you how our widget will take care of your other concerns, which are product compatibility and ongoing maintenance."

3. Confirm the next steps

The last part of the opening is to articulate the next steps you hope to take. This ensures that you and the prospects are on a level playing field and there are no misunderstandings or surprises. A statement such as, "I hope once you see a few of the advantages of our widgets, we can get together after the show for a more detailed presentation" will keep you both on track. Or if you expect an immediate sale, you might say, "Once you see the benefits of our new line, I would like you to consider adding it to your existing inventory."

You have just told prospects what you are going to tell them. You have also created the outline for the body of your presentation.

Think about your next show appearance. Spend a few minutes creating an effective opening for a booth presentation.

The opening_____

_____

The bridge_____

_____

Confirming the need_____

_____

Confirming the next step_____

_____

_____

e. *THE BODY: "TELL THEM"*

1. A methodical approach

The body of your presentation matches the individual needs expressed by your prospects to your product or service. Introduce one need at a time and your presentation won't jump around. This provides a logical flow and makes it easier for prospects to focus. A methodical approach helps you create maximum impact. This isn't a televised football game. Your prospects don't have the advantage of an instant replay if they miss an important point. It's your job to keep them on track and focused.

Don't fall into the trap of telling prospects all about your product without getting some feedback. You could be spinning your wheels and wasting time. A good way to start is by asking a simple question such as, "What are you looking for in a coffee cup?" This should bring a specific answer such as, "Well, I need a cup that's good looking and not expensive."

With this question you have identified two areas of need: appearance and cost. Before addressing these needs, you should explore further to see if the prospect has any other needs. You can do this by repeating the first two needs and asking a further simple question such as the following.

- For the visual: "You want a coffee cup that is not only attractive but inexpensive. Is there anything else that you are looking for in a cup?"

- For the auditory: "Tell me what else it should have."

- For the kinesthetic: "What do you feel is also important in a cup?"

Now you can proceed to satisfy each need with a benefit statement about your product. But you still need to make sure that prospects have understood the information you have given them. The only way to do this is by checking back. Constant feedback through the presentation is the key to gaining and maintaining prospect commitment. After each benefit has been introduced, you should check back.

- For the visual you will say: "Does that look like a fit?"

- For the auditory: "Does that sound about right?"

- For the kinesthetic: "Does that feel right?"

Checking back after you introduce each benefit will keep you both on the same track and help you avoid the shopping list syndrome. The shopping list syndrome is when poorly prepared salespeople tell prospects everything they can think of. All the features and benefits are listed with the hope that something will be important. Or worse yet, they assume that everything *is* important and tell prospects the whole story.

Deal with each need by stating the feature then following quickly with the benefit. Next add a quick proof statement and a confirmation that the information is understood and of value to your prospect. Finally, bridge to the next need.

This process goes something like this: "Our kryptonite-based (feature) widget will help you achieve the economies you are looking for (benefit). We have had considerable success with other manufacturers in your industry and have been able to show them as much as a 53% decrease in costs (proof). Are these the kind of results you are looking for?"

If prospects are satisfied, your bridge sounds like this: "The other area you are concerned about is compatibility. Let me show you how our interchangeable parts makes compatibility a concern of the past."

2. Features and benefits

Features are the actual characteristics of a product or service. Benefits are what those features mean to customers. Imagine, for example, you are selling a line of coffee cups. The features of this cup are shape, material, design, a hole in the lid, and a handle. If you are selling a service, the features are a list of the components. In the travel industry, features are things such as "all inclusive," "modified American plan," transfers, double occupancy, excursion, and complimentary cocktails.

To excite your prospects, you must also sell the benefit that goes with the feature, otherwise you are liable to get a ho-hum reaction. "So what?" your customer says, "What's so special about that? I've seen a million more like 'em," or "That sounds like last year's holiday."

Features are "so what?" statements. If you give prospects a list of features and leave your presentation there, you have completed only half your job. A good benefit statement tells simply and clearly what a particular feature will do for the prospects:

230

"This cup has a well-balanced handle that makes it easier to hold when full, and it is insulated so your coffee stays hot longer."

"Hey, that's just what I've been looking for!" exclaims the customer. You have made your sale.

Here are two more examples:

Feature: Our personal computer comes complete with a 200 MHZ processor, 64-bit accelerated graphics, and 2 MB video, 32 MB, and 16X CD-ROM with a 512K pipeline. Not to mention the 33.6K/14.4K bps data/fax modem.

Benefits: The 200 MHZ process gives you the power and speed to use almost all programs on the market today. The 32MB lets you use any memory intensive multi-media software and the CD-ROM and 512K pipeline puts you ahead of the crowd.

Feature: Our bank offers overdraft protection.

Benefits: You will never be embarrassed by having a bounced cheque if you accidentally overdraw your account.

3. Proofs

Introducing features and benefits is a beginning. Proving your statements is the next step. A good proof statement is one that convinces prospects that their need has been met. You can find proof in testimonials, articles, industry statistics, research, and case studies. Prepare your proof sources ahead of time so they can be introduced at the appropriate times. For example, to introduce a proof you might say, "The AMA has given this product its highest recommendation."

Next, make sure you are still on the right track. Having a dozen benefits lined up doesn't mean your prospects will be excited about all of them. You need to find out which benefits strike a favorable note and concentrate on those.

By constantly looking for reinforcement and asking questions, you keep prospects involved and ensure the proofs are meaningful. If prospects don't agree with the proof source you have quoted, use another. This is why you will quote only one proof source at a time. Beware of the pitfall of overselling.

If prospects do agree, bridge to the next area of concern with a simple statement such as, "Now let me deal with the compatibility issue."

By handling one concern at a time, you avoid the danger of having your prospect bogged down in detail. If you have done your job well, a post-show meeting can be arranged to spend the proper amount of time needed to review all the details. Or, you can proceed to close the sale now. It all depends on your show objective.

Think for a moment about your own products and services. What are all the features and what are the benefits that go with each of these features?

All salespeople should complete this exercise with all their products and services. Write down your features and benefits and they will be fixed in your mind and easier to recall.

Another worthwhile exercise is to do the same thing for your competitor's products and services. Construct this list from your prospects' point of view. When you are faced with objections from prospects as they compare your product with your competitor's down the aisle, you will be in a good position to handle these objections. (Objections are discussed in section 4, below.)

Take a moment to fill in Worksheet #3. List five features of one of your products or services. Then list the relevant benefits and proof sources. Now do the same thing for a similar product or service sold by your competitor.

If you are not sure about your competition, shows are a good place to find out more about them.

4. Handling objections

Ouch! What if your prospects say no and don't agree with you? Don't panic. Objections are what many inexperienced salespeople fear. However, objections are nothing more than negative comments about your product or service.

Often, objections are a prospect's way of telling you that he or she has unsatisfied needs. Seasoned professionals look forward to objections, because when handled skillfully, sales are within sight.

When you hear an objection, the first rule is to stay calm. Dealing with objections effectively requires being well prepared. Have a bull session with your colleagues before the show, with some playing the role of devil's advocate and raising all the objections they can think of. In this way, you will hone your skills, anticipate some of the objections you are likely to run into, and be able to calmly handle them.

Worksheet #3
Features, benefits, and proofs

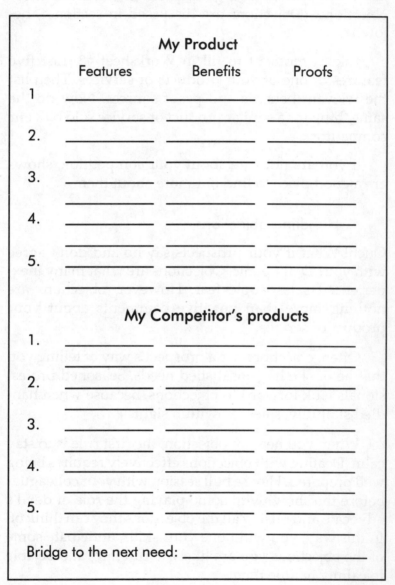

My Product

	Features	Benefits	Proofs
1			
2.			
3.			
4.			
5.			

My Competitor's products

1.			
2.			
3.			
4.			
5.			

Bridge to the next need: _____

What are you dealing with?

"It's too expensive!"

"I'll show you a cheaper one," the salesperson volunteers as he proceeds to move the customer around the shop looking for a product that works within the customer's budget.

This strategy may work in a normal situation, but it won't at a show. Consider the opportunities walking by your booth as you try to find something that will make this prospect happy.

When prospects object to the price, what are they really saying? They may think the price is too high, it could be they can't afford it, or it could be that they simply don't understand the features of your product and therefore don't see the value. Also consider that prospects could be putting up smoke screens to hide their real objections.

Your first response to an objection should simply be to ask the prospect if there is anything else that he or she hasn't told you. "So you are concerned about the price. Is there anything else that concerns you?" This way you get all the problems out in the open quickly and can deal with them one by one.

Here's another approach: "You're concerned that our product seems too expensive. May I ask you what you are comparing us to?"

Once you have this information you can go to work. If you have done your homework, you know the benefits of your competitor's products. You can answer something like this: "You said you were concerned about extended warranties. Does ABC company offer the warranty you are looking for?" (Assuming that you have done your homework, you know that it doesn't or you wouldn't ask this question.)

If it looks as though the objection will take a long time to deal with, it may be better to put it off until after the show: "Mr. Prospect, you've brought up a good point, and I'd like to show you in detail how our machine can overcome the problem you mention. To do that, I need to spend some time with you when we can both relax and examine this thoroughly in a less hectic environment. I would like to come to your office next week to explain everything. What would be a good day for you, Tuesday or Wednesday?"

List the objections you are likely to hear at a show a create a list of your answers.

Objection_____

_____

_____

Response_____

_____

_____

f. THE CLOSE: "TELL THEM WHAT YOU HAVE JUST TOLD THEM"

Handled properly, your closing sets up a number of important steps. It confirms that prospects are interested, it sets the tone for some follow-up activities, and it helps you disengage.

1. Restate the need

The close starts with a quick review of prospects' needs and the features and benefits of your products or services. It is not necessary to restate proofs. If you are wondering whether this repetition is necessary, it is. Repetition is a key learning principle. Your summary puts your whole discussion into a nice package and makes it easy for prospects to make decisions.

An example of restating the need is: "I've shown you how our new widget effectively handles the problem of compatibility, and I've shown you how our post-sale service package will ensure your requirements for on-going maintenance."

2. Ask for a commitment

The second step is to ask for a commitment. Prospects already know what you are going to ask for because you took the time to prepare them in your opening. Asking for a commitment is a great way to ease into an effective disengagement. You might say, "The next step is for us to schedule a time to get together to reexamine the whole picture. When would be a good time to do that?" or "Let's put together a sample order now."

3. Reinforce rapport

The final move is to leave the prospect with a good feeling about you and the relationship you have just initiated. For example: "I am looking forward to meeting you on the 15th. It has been great meeting you, and I hope you enjoy the rest of the show" or "If you have any questions once you get this back to your office, I am no farther away than the nearest phone."

You are now free to look for other prospects.

Complete your presentation in the space below.

The close_____

_____

Restate the need_____

_____

Ask for the commitment_____

_____

Reinforce rapport_____

_____

An effective show presentation is the heart of the sales interaction at a show. Good planning, effective time management, and flexibility will make your presentations direct, meaningful, and, most of all, profitable.

There may be more than one presentation that you will make at a show. Use Worksheet #4 to create an alternate presentation for your next show.

4. Closing the sale

If the first stages in the selling process have been followed correctly, closing should be a natural final step. Unfortunately, for many this is where the sale is lost. I have seen willing prospects actually be talked out of buying by salespeople who don't know when to stop talking. Instead of writing the orders and thanking customers for the business, the salespeople continue to present the product and lose the sale by annoying the prospects.

The opening

The bridge _____

_____

Confirm the need _____

_____

Confirm the next steps _____

_____

The body

Need #1

Bridge _____

Feature _____

Benefit _____

Proof _____

Confirm _____

Bridge _____

Need #2

Bridge _____

Feature _____

Benefit_____

Proof _____

Confirm _____

Bridge _____

Handling objections

Possible objections   Answers

_____   _____

_____   _____

_____   _____

The close

Restate the need _____

_____

Ask for a commitment _____

_____

Reinforce rapport _____

_____

Some salespeople hesitate to close because they fear a negative reply. They hate to hear the word NO. To them, a negative response means the prospects haven't liked the product or service, have rejected their ideas and indirectly them. That's a pretty heavy burden.

However, salespeople should know that a negative answer can mean other things, such as:

- "You haven't given me enough information to decide."

- "You didn't listen to what I told you earlier, and you haven't cleared up my objections."

- "I'm not interested now, but I will be interested at a later date."

- "I never say yes the first time . . . ask me again."

Whatever the true motive behind the negative answer, experienced salespeople know not to take it personally. Your challenge is to find the true cause of the negative answer and do something about it. That's what selling is all about. So, if you view closing as an act of confirming with your prospect that you are on the right track, the burden disappears and you can close with confidence.

Here are the five rules for closing:

(a) If you don't ask, you won't get the order.

(b) Before you ask, make sure you know what you are asking for.

(c) It's better to be a little early than a whole lot late.

(d) Always have a back-up goal.

(e) Always get a commitment.

(a) Buying signals

Some salespeople are determined to give a complete presentation regardless of the buying signals prospects are transmitting. Here's a good example of this scenario that I happened to overhear at a recent show. The salesperson qualified the prospect well and began his presentation. After a while, the prospect said, "This is the first time I've seen your product and I'm really impressed."

"Thank you," the salesperson said, "but don't let me forget to tell you about the warranty that comes with each purchase." Whereupon he launched into a detailed description of the warranty package.

"Well, I'm convinced," the prospect interjected.

"Good, it's also important to understand the packaging of this item which has been designed to . . . "

Finally the prospect insisted, "How do I order some?"

At this point the salesperson finally got the message and pulled out his order pad.

If you had spoken to this salesperson afterward, he would have insisted that he had closed the sale. He would not have acknowledged that it was, in reality, the customer who had forced the close. By his insensitivity, this salesperson not only risked losing the sale but also wasted valuable time that could have resulted in additional sales with other prospects.

What are buying signals? Buying signals are gestures, movements, and words that prospects will use to let you know they have been persuaded. Buying signals can be seen through your keen observations. If you watch your prospects closely you will see specific changes in their behavior that can be interpreted as indications to you to change what you are doing.

These changes can be subtle. After all, the chances of prospects saying, "Okay, I'm convinced, sell me something" are pretty slim. You will notice a change in their facial coloring, a shifting of their body stance, and a refocusing of their eyes.

In chapter 10 we discussed how people process information. You learned that we are all unique in what we do with what is being told to us. You now understand how people react to information that is presented properly, and information that is foreign to their method of processing data. By watching for changes, and understanding the differences between people who are visual, auditory, and kinesthetic, you will be able to spot buying signals. Moreover, you will be able to proceed properly with each prospect you meet. Be patient and know that before you are ready to close, you had better refer back to your objective.

(b) If you don't ask . . . you won't get the order

As I said earlier, time is of the essence, and you can't wait too long to close the sale. Each minute you waste, some 15 to 20 other prospects have passed by your booth.

(c) Before you ask, make sure you know what you're asking for

This rule refers back to the discussion in chapter 1 of setting goals for the show. If your goal is to make sales, ask for the order.

- *For the visual:*

  "Would you like to see this delivered by the end of the week?" or

  "Can you picture your results with our new process?"

- *For the auditory:*

  "It sounds like we've got the solution for you," or

  "Does that ring any bells for you?"

- *For the kinesthetic:*

  "Do you have a firm grasp on the benefits of installation?" or

  "It all boils down to one simple answer, yes or no."

If your goal is to get qualified leads, ask for information.

- *For the visual:*

  "Once you see the results, I would like to talk about plant-wide implementation," or

  "If it's the monochrome look you are looking for, we've got the solution."

- *For the auditory:*

  "Your board will surely respond positively to these cost saving measures" or

  "After you have received our proposal, I would like to talk to you further."

- *For the kinesthetic:*

  "Sifting through all the options can be confusing" or

244

"Once you have samples in your hands, you will be able to make the right decision."

If your goal is to set up appointments, ask for the appointment.

- *For the visual:*

    "It looks like we've got what you need. Let's set up a time to look at all the options" or

    "You and I should get together to develop a clear-cut plan of action."

- *For the auditory:*

    "Something tells me this is the right product for you. The next step is for you and me to discuss the details" or

    "Let's get together next week where we will not be interrupted by the noisy distractions of the show."

- *For the kinesthetic:*

    "I have a feeling that we've got a good fit here. When we meet again we can iron out any wrinkles" or

    "In the calmness of your office, with a minimum of interruption, I will be better able to demonstrate how our product will blend into your process."

What if you misinterpret the buying signal and close too early?

This is a real concern and often a cause for holding back. It shouldn't be, as you'll learn from the third rule of closing.

(d) It's better to be a little early than a whole lot late

You need to find the balance between being too pushy and being assertive by asking for what you want. Mastery of this technique comes with experience. Seasoned professionals learn to sense when their prospects are ready to buy; they instinctively recognize the signals and ask for the close. They weren't born with this skill but learned it in the school of hard knocks where trial and error is the teacher.

To develop a sense of timing, you must try and try again. Don't worry about making a mistake. If you make a mistake, with some planning, you can work your way out of most situations. Here's an example:

"So, Ms. Prospect, it sounds as if this is the product for you."

"Not so fast! I'm not ready to buy from you, or anyone else, yet."

"Oh, is there something else you would like this product to do?"

You see, it's quite easy to turn a negative response into an opportunity to uncover more information. With this new information, you are better armed to move the prospect closer to closing.

(e) Always have a back-up goal

So far, we've assumed that your prospects will fall in line with the goal you have set for your company and yourself. For instance, you may have a company goal of $20,000 in sales, which breaks down into a personal goal for each salesperson of $5,000 for the show, or 20 sales

246

of $250 each. This may be a good goal for the type of product or service you are selling, but what if it doesn't fit with the prospects' requirements? Suppose a prospect says, "Yes, it's the kind of merchandise I think will work in my store, but I'd like to sample it first with a smaller order of $100, and see how it works out."

In this scenario, unless you have a minimum order requirement or some other constraint, you accept the order even though it falls short of your personal goal. The successful salesperson always has a fall-back position in case the original goal cannot be met.

The fall-back position in this scenario was a lower dollar amount. Other positions you may choose could be an alternative appointment date, an introduction to the person with real buying authority, a testimonial, a promise to receive and review some literature, or another call.

(f) Always get a commitment

Don't be caught off guard if your original goal is unattainable. Find something your prospect can realistically commit to. Always get a commitment in some form from the prospect before ending the presentation. Having qualified the prospect, made your full presentation, and answered objections, you must strive to get a commitment, otherwise your efforts will have been wasted. If you can't make a sale today, make a follow-up appointment, confirm it, and make the sale tomorrow.

14

DISENGAGING

Once you have established that your visitor does not qualify for your products or services, or your visitor qualifies and you have made a presentation and closed, there is one more important step to take. Wrap up the conversation effectively so you can move on to the next prospect.

Effective time management is your most valuable asset. There is nothing wrong with spending extra time with a visitor during low-traffic times.

However, during high-traffic times you will be missing important opportunities if you continue talking long after you have met your objective. You also are not respecting your prospect's time to see the rest of the show. Once your job is done, move on.

Disengaging does not have to be rude or impolite. It is the logical end to a conversation and, if handled properly, leaves the visitor with a positive feeling about you, your company, and its products.

But you need to effectively disengage while staying focused on your objective. Once it has been achieved, it's time to move on. Develop the skill to end the conversation gracefully and when you want to.

Disengaging is easy: you agree on a follow-up, thank the visitor for his or her time, shake hands, and move on: "Mr. Smith, it has been great meeting you today. I'll get that information out to you as soon as I return to my office and then I'll call to set up an appointment. Thanks for your interest and enjoy the rest of the show."

Disengaging can, at times, present a real challenge. Some visitors will chat all day if you let them. Remember, by letting them continue to talk, you are squandering time, both yours and theirs. So, how do you get yourself ready to disengage?

a. THE THREE P'S OF DISENGAGING

1. Promptly

You have to disengage when the time is right. Delaying, as you already know, is a waste of time. Often there is an uncomfortable silence that indicates the conversation is over. There can be both verbal and non-verbal signals. The prospect may say, "Let me think about it," or "Give me your card and I'll get back to you," or the prospect may start to shuffle his or her feet, look bored or impatient, or take a step back from you. Often the prospect will not know how to disengage, so it is up to you to take the initiative.

2. Professionally

Professionalism is a word often abused. We recognize that doctors, lawyers, and engineers are professionals, but in the term "sales professional," professional is used loosely. A sales professional is one who has developed skills of finding the right solution for the right problem.

You need to find the people you can help, understand their needs, and come up with the right solution.

As a sales professional your time is just as valuable as your doctor's or lawyer's. Over your professional life you have developed skills that have helped you become successful. And, like other professionals, you are continually learning new skills to help you become better. Reading this book is a good example.

If you really consider yourself to be a professional, handle people professionally. Once your job is done, disengage quickly. Hanging on long after you have made the sale or set up a future appointment is truly a waste. No other professional would do it. Neither should you.

3. Properly

All skills must be done properly to be effective. Disengaging is polite and an expected activity.

There are various techniques you can use. Some common disengagement techniques are explained in the sections below. Try them at your next show.

b. DISENGAGEMENT TECHNIQUES

1. Disengaging from qualified prospects using a premium

Premiums, draws, literature, and sampling are great tools to help you disengage. The trick is to use them strategically. Premiums, for example, should never be placed out in the open for every passerby to pick up (see chapter 5 on handling premiums). Rather, premiums should be hidden from view and given out at the appropriate time. One of these times is when you need to disengage.

Follow these three steps and you will end the conversation in a friendly and professional manner.

(a) Step #1: Change the mood

It is important to stop talking about business and give the visitor some indication that the conversation is drawing to a close: "Mr. Smith, it has been great talking to you today" or "I hope that gives you a good idea about how our products can help you increase your efficiency."

(b) Step #2: The set-up

The second step is the set-up. Say something like, "Before you leave . . ." or "There is something I would like you to have as a reminder of our visit today."

(c) Step #3: The offer

The third step is the offer. This is your chance to offer visitors a chance to stay and look around your booth or to enter a draw for a prize that only someone who is truly interested in your product would want to win.

"Mr. Smith, we are giving each of our new customers this special pen, with our thanks. I am looking forward to meeting you next week to discuss our product further. I hope you enjoy the rest of the show."

"Mr. Smith, I will send that literature to you immediately and I will follow up with a phone call to see if you need any further information."

"You have sampled our new product. How about one more for the road?"

"Mr. Smith, before you go why don't you take a moment to enter our draw, you have a chance to win gift certificate for . . . "

How would you disengage from a qualified prospect?

_____

_____

_____

_____

2. Disengaging from unqualified people without using a premium

Sometimes you may not have a tangible gift for visitors. Following the three steps outlined above in section 1. and offering an intangible can be equally as effective:

"Mr. Smith, it has been great talking to you today. Before you leave, please take a moment to look around our booth and see if there is anything that interests you. If you need more information, let me know. It has been nice meeting you and I hope you enjoy the rest of the show."

"Just look at the time. There is a great workshop that starts in a few minutes and I know you will want to hear it."

The prospect will use this as an opening to leave. Why? Because he or she is part of the majority of show attendees who have an agenda. The prospect now knows that you do not have anything for them.

3. Disengaging while acknowledging the presence of other visitors

Looking over one prospect's shoulder for other prospects is bad manners. You can spot other people in your booth without breaking eye contact by using your peripheral vision. If you ignore these new prospects, they will leave. A quick acknowledgment will keep them there longer. This acknowledgment is an excellent bridge to begin disengaging from the prospect you are in a conversation with.

Break eye contact with the prospect by saying, "Mr. Smith, excuse me for a second." Then make eye contact with the new prospect, saying, "I'll be with you in a moment."

This not only keeps the second prospect a bit longer, it lets the first prospect know your conversation is drawing to a close.

If you are going to be longer than a quick minute, refer the new prospect to the video, demonstration, or some product information that will keep him or her busy until you have time to get to that prospect.

How would you handle this situation?

_____

_____

_____

_____

4. Disengaging from your existing customers

Occasionally customers will drop by just to chat. These people are not ready to upgrade or buy more product — they just want to chat.

These customers deserve some of your time and should be treated with care. However, spending booth time with them will not help you meet your show objectives. The best disengagement here is an honest one. Explain the situation and find some time more convenient to have your conversation:

"Mr. Smith, what a surprise to see you today. I'm really interested in hearing all about how the new product has helped your production, but I've got a problem. At this show we are expecting over 10,000 visitors and many will be dropping by our booth. You and I won't be able to get into a conversation without being interrupted. I'm taking a break at two o'clock. Why don't I buy you a cup of coffee then and we can spend some time together?"

There is nothing wrong with a direct, honest approach. You have already established a relationship with your customers and once you explain the situation, they will understand.

How would you disengage from existing customers?

_____

_____

_____

_____

5. Disengaging from a complainer

We all dread having to face someone with a complaint, whether the complaint is legitimate or not. Although it is understood that the complainer has a need to be heard, airing complaints on the show floor is not the best place for him or her to do so.

So how do you deal with this type of situation? You must first let the complainer know you are listening and then quickly disengage with a strategy similar to the one used with existing customers — honesty:

"Mrs. Brown, I am really pleased that you have brought this to my attention. The problem you have is not acceptable and I want to deal with this one personally.

However, we are expecting over 10,000 visitors at this show and run the risk of being interrupted. I'm afraid I won't be able to deal with your problem now, but I will give you a call next Tuesday and we can discuss it in detail then. Would that be okay?"

Then bring out your appointment book and show the complainant you are writing down your commitment to call. This strategy should take care of most complainants.

In a small number of cases your first approach may not work. The complainer's anger or frustration may start to escalate. They may say, "Sure, after I leave the show I'll never hear from you again. I have already left dozens of unanswered voice-mail messages. You're here now and I want some action."

The escalation of this anger will be detrimental to the rest of your colleagues conducting business in the booth. So, get the complainer out of the booth as quickly as possible. You can not forcibly eject them, so say something like:

"Mrs. Brown, let's see if we can deal with this now. Let's go somewhere where we can talk privately and see if we can sort this out."

Signal your colleagues to let them know you are leaving the booth for a minute and take the complainer to a quiet area of the show to handle the problem.

How would you handle a complainer?

_____

_____

_____

_____

6. Disengaging from students

Local colleges and schools send students to shows to develop their knowledge and contacts. A show is a great opportunity for students to learn, network, and grow. If you focus on the big picture, you know that the longevity of your industry depends on young, new people with fresh ideas. Some student inquiries are welcome, but often they arrive when you are busy and become an interference. The way to handle this situation is with a simple explanation, one that does not put the student down:

"Beth, I would love to be able to give you some help, but you have arrived at a peak time. I know that later in the afternoon it gets quieter. Why don't you come back then when the chances of being interrupted are less."

If the student is serious (and this is the student you will want to spend time with), he or she will return. If the student isn't serious, you have lost nothing.

How would you disengage from a student?

_____

_____

_____

_____

7. Disengaging from other exhibitors

Exhibitors should not visit other exhibitors' booths unless they are invited. This is basic show etiquette. The boothers' first priority is to the attendees. If other exhibitors are getting in the way, disengage quickly:

"Joe, as you can see, we have a lot of visitors. Please excuse me for now. Perhaps we can get together later?"

How would you disengage from an exhibitor?

_____

_____

_____

_____

Disengaging doesn't come naturally, it requires practice. If you ignore this step you will be under-utilizing your show's potential. Like all new skills it will take time to become proficient. To overcome the barrier of time, make sure you are spending it wisely. Develop good approaching, qualifying, presenting, and engaging skills and your time will be well spent.

Information gathering in an environment where time is at a premium is your most important job at a show. Use the job aid (Worksheet #5) to plan your next show.

c. CONCLUSION

Working the booth is nothing more than developing skills to gather information in a situation where time is an obstacle. By understanding the three barriers to building rapport — time, fatigue, and attitude — you can improve your show appearance. Time is handled by the information gathering process; understanding your objective, approaching strangers, qualifying them quickly, making an effective presentation, and disengaging. Fatigue is minimized by finding methods of coping with yours and your prospects' fatigue by respecting their time.

And the right attitude is projected by understanding some simple skills that will help you say to visitors, "I'm the kind of person you want to do business with."

You are now ready to move on to the next chapter, where you will learn how to uncover the hidden opportunities at shows.

Worksheet #5
Information gathering job aid

Your approach

When visitors appear interested _____

_____

_____

During a demonstration

    a) *When you are working the booth*_____

_____

_____

    b) *When you are the demonstrator*_____

_____

_____

When nobody stops at the booth_____

_____

_____

Qualifying

Authority _____

_____

Capability_____

_____

Time_____

_____

Identity_____

_____

Obstacles_____

_____

Need_____

_____

The presentation

The opening

The bridge_____

_____

Confirm the need_____

_____

Confirm the next steps_____

_____

The body

Need #1

    Bridge_____

    Feature_____

    Benefit_____

    Proof _____

Confirm_____

Bridge_____

Need #2

Bridge_____

Feature_____

Benefit_____

Proof_____

Confirm _____

Bridge_____

Handling objections

Possible objections   Answers

_____   _____

_____   _____

_____   _____

The close

Restate the need _____

_____

Ask for a commitment_____

_____

Reinforce rapport_____

_____

Disengage

From a qualified prospect_____

_____

From an unqualified prospect _____

_____

Acknowledging the presence of another visitor_____

_____

From an existing customer_____

_____

From a complainer_____

_____

From a student_____

_____

From another exhibitor _____

_____

PART III
AFTER THE SHOW

15

FOLLOW-UP IS THE PAYOFF

If you collected a thousand leads at a show and didn't follow up on them, what use would they be? None at all. In fact, your months of effort in planning, attending, qualifying, and collecting those leads would have been wasted. Yet many companies do a poor job of following up the leads they collect at shows.

An effective follow-up system should be as carefully planned as the rest of your show activities — and should be done at the same time. When you know that you have a good follow-up system in place, then your qualifying and lead-collecting activities at the show take on far more meaning and urgency.

Another important consideration is your potential customers. Put yourself in their place. If you properly qualified the person as a *Ready Buyer*, gave a full sales presentation, and sent the person away with a promise to make contact after the show, you probably created considerable excitement and expectation in his or her mind. What's more, the customer probably spent time comparing your products with those of your competitors and left the show with a good idea of what he or she wanted to buy.

In order to clinch this sale, you must follow-up immediately while the excitement is still alive and before your competitors grab the order.

If you wait more than a week, the chances are that the prospect will have cooled off and may have placed the order elsewhere.

If you wait more than 30 days, you might as well throw the leads in the garbage.

Time is of the essence in any lead follow-up program. You must have a plan that allows you to contact all leads in some manner, as quickly as possible.

The following six points are the elements of a good lead follow-up program:

(a) Set a realistic goal for the number of leads you plan to collect during the show (see chapter 1).

(b) Design or use a lead-collecting system that makes recording and retrieval easy. If large numbers are expected, make sure that the system will generate mailing labels without a lot of extra effort.

(c) Plan your lead follow-up system well ahead of the show and have it ready to roll immediately after the show (see the discussion of methods that follows).

(d) Set deadlines for all follow-up activities and brief all staff on the importance of meeting deadlines and their individual roles in the project.

(e) Set up a system to record and review results of your follow-up program.

(f) Set a date for the final review.

There are three methods of follow-up: direct mail, telemarketing, and personal sales calls.

Many companies use more than one method. What you use will depend on your market, the number of leads you collected, and the promises made by your staff during the show. Let's take a more detailed look at the role that each of these methods can play in your follow-up activities.

a. DIRECT MAIL

If you receive a large number of leads, direct mail offers the quickest way of getting in touch with your prospects in the shortest time. As with all of your other show activities, your mailing program should be carefully planned with realistic goals and firm deadlines.

Your first mailing could be a simple letter thanking the prospect for visiting your booth and confirming the benefits of your product that were explained at that time. For a speedier reply you could send the letter by facsimile. Close the letter by promising a more personal contact in the near future or send a reply-paid card for use if fast action is required.

By sending such a letter, you have not only let prospects know that you value their interest in your product, but you have also gained a little more time in which to follow up with a personal call or a tele-marketing call to arrange a definite appointment. At this time, you should fulfill any promises that you made to the client.

Next, you should create a series of mailings at intervals, set to suit your business. The contents of the mailings would vary from letters and press releases to specification sheets, catalogues, and flyers offering special deals. A great deal of creativity goes into the designing of mailing pieces. They should be designed to grab the reader's attention as discussed in chapter 5. Keep a file of flyers you receive in the mail — they will be a constant source of new ideas for your own efforts.

b. TELEMARKETING

The object of telemarketing is to make personal contact with the prospect. It also allows you to get in touch with a large number of prospects in the space of a few days.

Here are some guidelines to good telemarketing.

(a) Use people who understand what they are selling, speak clearly, and have a pleasant telephone manner.

(b) Always identify the company. This serves two purposes: it tells the prospects who is calling — they are more likely to answer calls from companies they know than those they don't know; second, it serves as a constant reminder of your company name.

(c) If the telemarketer cannot answer a prospect's question, it should be noted and an answer provided within 24 hours if at all possible.

(d) Any promises made to a prospect should be logged, followed through, and reviewed by supervisors regularly.

(e) Use a bring-forward file to ensure that call-backs are made on the dates requested.

During the first contact, the telemarketer should thank the prospect for visiting your booth and quickly review your products and benefits. The telemarketer can then ask for an order, arrange an appointment for a salesperson to call, or arrange for the prospect to visit your show room. Later calls can introduce new products or new ideas, extend invitations to special events, or once again try to set up appointments.

c. PERSONAL SALES CALLS

Wherever possible, appointments should be made for personal calls. If you weren't able to fix a date at the show, then a phone call should be made either by the salesperson or by an experienced telemarketer. In the latter case, close cooperation between the salesperson and the telemarketer will be necessary to avoid conflicting appointments.

While setting up appointments is considered a common courtesy by many, you can't always get hold of people when you want to. If you are going to be in the area on a certain day, leave a message for the person saying you will try to contact him or her at that time. This approach has more chance of success than a straight cold call which many people regard as an unwarranted intrusion into their daily schedule.

By using a mix of each of these three methods, as determined by your particular situation, you can reap the full benefit of your efforts at the show and set the scene for an even more successful show next time.

16

POST-SHOW EVALUATION

Was it worth it? Should we do it again? What changes should we make? These are just three of the many questions you must answer once the show is over.

If you are to extract the full benefit from the show and maximize your investment, there are a number of things you should do in the days and weeks immediately following the show.

In chronological order, these things are —

(a) post-show debriefing,

(b) analysis of immediate results, and comparison with goals,

(c) final analysis of costs and results, and comparison with goals, and

(d) final report on show with recommendations for future shows.

These activities can be divided into two broad groups, subjective and statistical evaluations, each of which plays an important part in your overall assessment of the show.

Subjective evaluations tell you why and how things happened. They can come from a wide variety of people including your own staff, show staff, customers, competitors, and show visitors.

Statistical evaluations give you hard numbers against which you can compare your goals. They will come from your own staff and also from show management.

a. POST-SHOW DEBRIEFING

For maximum value, this should take place as soon as the show is over. Some companies prepare special evaluation forms for their booth staff to fill out immediately. This is particularly useful when staff have been drawn from different geographical locations and there is little probability of getting them all together again until the next show.

Other companies handle the debriefing by having a staff meeting, at which time evaluation forms may be filled out followed by a general discussion and recommendations for future shows.Whatever method is chosen, the review should take place while memories are still fresh in people's minds. A record of the comments and recommendations should be made for future use.

In addition to your own staff, valuable feedback can also be obtained from your customers and other visitors. You can do this by talking to them on the phone, sending them a questionnaire, inviting a representative group to a breakfast or luncheon meeting to discuss the show, or by employing an independent research company to do a survey for you.

Other sources of useful feedback are show managers, show services, competitors, and other exhibitors.

If you decide to prepare a questionnaire for your booth staff or others, it should be carefully thought out and structured. Here's a list of subjects that you might want to include in your questionnaire:

(a) Pre-show activities

Planning

Promotion

Training

Discussion of goals

Travel arrangements

Move-in

(b) At the show

Staffing and scheduling, technical back-up

Quality of booth

Comparison with competition

Caliber of demonstrations and displays

Staff knowledge, ability to answer questions

Staff behavior

Achievement of corporate goals

Literature and other materials

Signs and graphics

Lighting, floor coverings, location

Accessibility, show services, concessions

Traffic, audience quality

Registration and follow-up system

Any surprises?

Non-customer activities (students, agents, etc.)

Tear-down and move-out

(c) Post-show

Return and storage of booth

Lead follow-up

Accuracy and reliability of statistical data

Plans for next show

Overall impressions and recommendations

Since you are asking people for their thoughts and feelings, don't forget to express your appreciation for the time and effort that people spend.

b. ANALYSIS OF IMMEDIATE RESULTS

You should review the results immediately after the show and compare them with the goals that were set.

If your primary goal was to make sales at the show, count the sales. Your immediate follow-up action will be to make sure that all orders are dispatched without delay. If this is not possible, then customers should be notified of the delivery date and the order confirmed.

Where lead collecting was the primary goal, you should have a stack of lead cards or print-outs from the registration system. Whether you convert these leads into firm orders depends very much on your follow-up procedures (see chapter 15). However, your purpose at this moment is to compare the results statistically with your goals set before the show.

In preparing your statistics, you may find it helpful to sort the leads into several categories that match your goals. These might be —

(a) literature or catalogue requests,

(b) technical back-up,

(c) immediate buyer,

(d) medium-term buyer, and

(e) long-term buyer.

Compare the number of leads with the goals you set in different categories.

c. FINAL ANALYSIS OF COSTS AND RESULTS

Some weeks or months after the show, depending on your sales cycle, you should be able to bring together all of your costs and the full results from the show. These should be tabulated against your goals and budget for each item.

In addition to comparing the results with your goals, you should also be able to come up with statistics that will indicate how successful the show was for your company. By comparing your results with non-show sales costs, you will have a good yardstick by which to measure your current performance and predict that of future shows. Here are some examples of the kind of statistics you should be looking for:

(a) Number of sales calls required to close a show lead

(b) Cost of obtaining each lead (or sale) at the show

(c) Cost of each sale made as a result of the show

You can compare these results with your non-show costs of everyday business activities such as:

(a) Number of regular sales calls required to make a sale

(b) Cost of obtaining a sales lead through advertising or other forms of promotion such as direct mail

(c) Cost of each sale made as a result of non-show sales activities

When computing any of the above costs (show or non-show), all relevant costs should be included, otherwise the results will be skewed and of little value. In particular, staff salaries and travel costs should be charged to the show budget and not buried in some other part of the marketing budget, as so often happens. The same applies to promotion and advertising.

Surveys have shown that the cost of obtaining a qualified lead at a show is about one-third of the cost of an industrial sales call. While these figures are averages, they do stress the importance of developing your own bench marks.

d. FINAL REPORT

Now is the time to bring together all of your information. This information should be summarized in one final report that will act as a guideline for planning future shows, setting goals, and determining which shows are effective and which shows you should pass up.

This final report should assess the following:

(a) The overall reaction of customers, staff, and others to your exhibit, highlighting strengths and weaknesses. Recommendations for extra training, new approaches, etc., should be included.

(b) Comparison of actual costs to budget. This will highlight areas of weakness in budget controls and give firmer figures on which to base the next budget.

(c) Comparison of actual results to corporate and individual goals. This will point out areas of weak performance and the need for additional planning. Any shortfalls should be honestly assessed in terms of your own performance. Don't take the easy way out and blame the show management — unless the shortfall is common to most exhibitors.

Use Worksheet #6 to assess your performance at the show. Never lose sight of the fact that a show — trade or consumer — is a business proposition from start to finish. Plan it, execute it, and review it as you would any other business activity. If your show is successful, then you'll know how to go on to greater success next time. If the show fails to meet your expectations, you'll know why, and, more important, you'll know whether or not to participate in that show again or, alternatively, what you need to do to be successful in future.

Worksheet #6
Final report

Show_____

Dates_____Location_____

Comments from: Strengths   Weaknesses

Customers_____   _____

Staff_____   _____

Others_____   _____

Recommendations_____   _____

_____   _____

Costs
(see Worksheet #2)

	Actual $	Budget $	Difference (+) or(-)
Space rental	_____	_____	_____
Design & construction	_____	_____	_____
Transportation	_____	_____	_____
Show services	_____	_____	_____
Personnel	_____	_____	_____
Advertising & promotion	_____	_____	_____
Miscellaneous	_____	_____	_____

Goals
(see Worksheet #1)

Results   Comments

1. _____   _____
2. _____   _____
3. _____   _____
4. _____   _____
5. _____   _____

17

CONCLUSION

The results of your show depend very much on you. You can achieve your corporate goals and chalk up a resounding success, or you can have a disappointing, unproductive marketing expense. Or it can be something in between these extremes.

Over 2,400 years ago, Sun Tzu wrote in *The Art of War* (edited by James Clavell, Delacorte, 1983) that the first rule of war is to plan your attack. "The general who wins a battle makes many calculations in his temple before the fight. The general who loses a battle makes but few calculations beforehand."

The same advice is applicable to exhibiting at trade and consumer shows.

Throughout this book, I have emphasized the importance of planning each stage of your show participation. Those who plan well in advance and have a firm understanding of what they are going to do and how they are going to do it will succeed.

Salespeople who appreciate the opportunities that shows offer approach shows with excitement and enthusiasm. Their attitude at the booth will make a big difference to your results. Properly trained booth staff will perform at their peak. These are the little things that give you a competitive edge.

Tzu comments on attitude that, "Whoever is first in the field and waits the coming of the enemy will be fresh for the fight; whoever is second in the field and has to hasten to battle will arrive exhausted."

Whether you meet your opponent on the battleground or the show floor, your needs are similar. To succeed, you must be ready.

Don't just read this book and file it away. Make it required reading for every member of your exhibition staff. Review it before each show.

Remember, a *Ready Buyer* is best met by a *Ready Seller*.

Good luck and excellent planning in all your future shows!

APPENDIX 1
TRADE SHOW DIRECTORIES

The following is a listing of trade show directories available in the United States and Canada covering domestic and international shows.

a. *UNITED STATES*

Tradeshow Week Data Book
Tradeshow Week
12333 W. Olympic Boulevard, Suite 236
Los Angeles, CA 90064
(213) 826-5696
Toll-free: 1-800-521-8110

Tradeshows & Exhibits Schedule
Successful Meetings DataBank
633 Third Avenue
New York, NY 10164-0635
(212) 973-4890
Toll-free: 1-800-253-6708

Health Care Industry Trade Show Directory
Paradata Research
2 Summer Street, Suite 14
Natick, MA 01760
(508) 655-7922

*Media Map: The Definitive Guide to Computer
Industry Trade Shows*
Media Map
130 Great Road
Bedford, MA 01730
(617) 275-5560

Tradeshow and Convention Guide
Amusement Business
P.O. Box 24970
Nashville, TN 37202
(615) 321-4250

b. CANADA

Business Events Guide
714 Chemin du Golf
Nuns' Island, Quebec
H3E 1A8
(514) 766-1000

Shows and Exhibitions
Maclean Hunter Ltd.
Maclean Hunter Building
777 Bay Street
Toronto, Ontario
M5W 1A7
(416) 596-6035

c. INTERNATIONAL

International Trade Fairs and Conference Directory
Co-Mar Management Services
8 King Street E., #1110
Toronto, Ontario
M5C 1B5
(416) 364-1223
Toll-free: 1-800-727-4183

The Exhibit Review
3800 S.W. Cedar Hills Boulevard, Suite 241
Beaverton, OR 97005
(503) 643-2783

Tradeshow Week Data Book International
12333 W. Olympic Boulevard, Suite 236
Los Angeles, CA 90064
(213) 826-5696
Toll-free: 1-800-521-8110

Trade Shows Worldwide
Gale Research, Inc.
835 Penobscot Building
Detroit, MI 48226-4094
Toll-free: 1-800-347-4253

Calendar of International Tradeshows and Exhibitions
TWI International Exhibition Logistics
3190 Clearview Way
San Mateo, CA 94402
(415) 573-6900

APPENDIX 2
ACTION PLAN

This plan is provided as a checklist of all the actions you need to take to bring off a successful exhibition from the preliminary planning stage through to the final review several weeks or months after the show.

a. PRELIMINARY PLANNING

- ❑ Identify goals.

- ❑ List markets or market segments you wish to reach.

- ❑ List shows that cover your market(s).

- ❑ Obtain information — demographics, dates, locations, prices, special events, etc., from the managers of shows that interest you.

- ❑ Tabulate comparable data for each of the shows that interest you.

- ❑ Determine what results you would like to get from exhibiting at one or more of these shows.

- ❑ Define your general objectives for the show(s).

- ❑ List product(s) or service(s) you would display or promote at the show.

- ❑ Identify any special manufacturing or importing required.

❑ Determine if you have sufficient lead time to get these items.

❑ Calculate how much booth space you would need.

❑ Estimate the number of people you will need to properly staff a booth this size.

❑ Calculate the cost.

❑ Prepare a draft budget for the show and compare it with the amount allocated in your overall budget for shows. Does it fit? If not, what compromises are necessary?

❑ Judge if you have enough information to confidently make a decision to proceed to the second stage of planning.

b. PRE-SHOW PLANNING

1. Make your plan

❑ Pick your show crew.

❑ Call a meeting to set firm objectives for the show.

❑ Determine how much booth space you'll need to meet these objectives.

❑ Confirm that your show crew is large enough to handle the project.

❑ Pick the show(s) that best serves your objectives.

❑ Set a theme for your exhibit and select items for display.

- ❏ Identify any special events you would like to host.

- ❏ Plan demonstrations, games, premiums, etc.

- ❏ Plan your advertising program.

- ❏ Choose a display company to design and build your booth.

- ❏ Plan your follow-up program.

2. Start the action

- ❏ Book your show space as soon as possible to get best location.

- ❏ Select booth design that meets your needs technically and financially.

- ❏ Order booth and set deadlines for final design, manufacture, and final approval.

- ❏ Start your advertising and promotion program. Wherever possible, integrate your promotion activities with those of show management and your trade magazines.

- ❏ With the aid of the exhibitor's guide from your chosen show manager, set up a chart showing deadlines for critical activities such as arranging transportation for crew and for your exhibit; ordering on-site services and tickets for special events.

- ❏ Arrange for show services including janitor, electrical, water, drayage, hotel rooms, parking, audiovisual, carpets, plants, furniture, lights, any other special requirements.

- ❑ Order items needed for display.
- ❑ Set up training program for booth staff.
- ❑ Design and order lead forms.
- ❑ Explain your lead follow-up program to your office staff and booth personnel.
- ❑ Coordinate your lead retrieval system with the show manager's registration system.
- ❑ Organize special events, demonstrations, press briefings, premiums, etc.
- ❑ Do a dry run to set up the booth (if practical), and train your crew before it is shipped.
- ❑ Pack and ship your display or check that display company has done so.
- ❑ Ship lead forms, literature, and general stationery items.
- ❑ Set up booth duty schedules.
- ❑ Make one final check that everything has been ordered.

c. AT THE SHOW

1. Before the show opens

❑ Check booth set-up.

❑ Check that everything works and all supplies are on hand.

❑ Hold final training sessions on boothmanship and qualifying.

❑ Review schedules with booth staff and iron out any last-minute difficulties.

❑ Meet the press and place releases (kits) in press room.

❑ Check at-the-show promotions.

❑ Check demonstrations and special events.

2. During the show

❑ Hold daily reviews of progress toward objectives.

❑ Make any changes necessary.

❑ Take time to check out what your competition is doing.

3. When the show closes

❑ Secure valuable items.

❑ Pack all display items.

❑ Collect leads and dispatch to processing center.

❑ Dismantle booth, pack, and ship.

❑ De-brief crew as soon as possible.

❑ Go out and have a relaxing evening.

d. *POST- SHOW ACTIVITIES*

1. Immediate post-show action

❑ Hold first evaluation meeting as soon as possible after the show before memories start to fade.

❑ Process your leads according to plan.

❑ Initiate active follow-up of leads.

❑ When your booth returns, check for damage and arrange storage.

2. In the weeks and months that follow

❑ Monitor follow-up program.

❑ Hold final review.

❑ Make recommendations for changes at future shows.

❑ Start plans for next show.